TARBUCK
ON SHOWBIZ

TARBUCK
ON SHOWBIZ

Illustrations by Richard Willson

Willow Books
Collins
Grafton Street, London
1985

To Alec Fyne, Val Parnell, Terry Miller, Mike Parkinson, David Bell
and Peter Prichard – 'cos they believed.

Willow Books
William Collins & Co Ltd
London Glasgow Sydney Auckland
Toronto Johannesburg

Tarbuck, Jimmy
Tarbuck on showbiz
1. Amusements – Anecdotes, facetiae, satire, etc.
I. Title
791'.0207 GV1201.3

ISBN 0 00 218190 8

Made by Lennard Books
Mackerye End, Harpenden
Herts AL5 5DR

Editor Michael Leitch
Designed by David Pocknell's Company Ltd
Production Reynolds Clark Associates Ltd
Printed and bound in Great Britain by
Butler & Tanner Ltd,
Frome, Somerset

CONTENTS

INTRODUCTION

'A funny way to be a hero.' That was how someone described the life of a comedian. I agree. At times the whole of show business defies analysis, and this book is one of those times.

Show business is a kind of club. If you succeed, the rewards and the sense of personal fulfilment can be immense. As Ted Ray said: 'Don't tell people about it, or they'll want to do it.'

Personality is always important in show business, and in general you can say that the more generous a person is, the better he or she will do in their career. Unfortunately, there is a type of performer who suffers severely from 'I' complex, and this is a cross that the rest of us must bear. I met one not long ago in Langan's restaurant in London. He was a comic.

'Oh,' he said, 'I was in Blackpool last Sunday. I paralyzed them. I did two hours in Northampton on the Monday – I had them cheering and shouting for more. Tuesday it was Coventry. Wonderful, I can't tell you. The write-ups – I've never seen anything to compare. I was in Birmingham on the Wednesday . . .'

I said: 'That's right. I saw you.'

'Oh,' he said quickly. 'I didn't do too well there . . .'

There are no qualifications for entering show business – only a willingness to stand up and shoot them before they get you. Whether you are a dancer, a comic, or you command a flock of pigeons that fly backwards eating liquorice allsorts, it obviously pays to be quick on your feet. So, here and now, let me nominate the Finest Ad-Lib I have ever heard.

It was made by the late wonderful Diana Dors on the Russell Harty Show. She was appearing with Omar Sharif. Russell wanted to know why Sharif was not married any more. He explained:

'One morning, my wife and I woke up in bed and found it was no longer exciting. Being civilized people, we parted.'

'Fancy,' said Russell and turned to Diana. 'Can you imagine, Miss Dors, anything worse than being in bed with Omar Sharif and finding it not exciting any more?'

Diana said: 'Yes. Being in bed with you and finding it was.'

It undoubtedly takes all sorts, and even among the top management you find people with surprising gaps in their knowledge. As Leslie Grade settled into his chair in the sumptuous restaurant, the Maître d' glided up with enormous leather-bound menus.

Maître d': 'May I suggest the Châteaubriand?'

Leslie Grade: 'No, let's get the food ordered before the wine.'

That may give you an idea of the book that follows – an unceremonious tour of show business, the facts *and* the fantasies. We look at some wonderful variety acts, some stupefying disasters, some great moments in pantomime – including the finest get-out I have ever witnessed. We would have had a longer chapter on agents, but when they saw the material they insisted on taking out ten per cent. We look at the great comedians of the modern era, from Max Miller to Eric Morecambe, and I recall some special moments that I have spent with them. There are stories about Kenny Lynch scattered here and there; read them at your peril.

Finally, no guide to the institutions of show business would be complete without a behind-the-scenes Des O'Connor story. This one is about his perm.

Lennie Bennett talked him into having it done. And when I say 'it', it was an it. The first time I saw Des's perm was in Tramps one night after I had been doing a Michael Parkinson Show. It had been a great night, the adrenalin was still running, and when I saw this thing I had hysterics. If

ever a feller should not have had a perm, it was the delightful Des O'Connor.
I said: 'Whatever is that thing on your head?'
Des has a quick wit and usually comes back with a good reply. This time he gave me the Lamest Ad-lib I have ever heard. He said:
'I've had it done because I've been doing a lot of swimming.'
I said to him: 'Desdemona! You've got to do better than that.'
He agreed. And it's true. No-one can win them all. I have just told two stories which I have labelled the Finest Ad-lib and the Lamest. Somewhere between the two lies the real story of show business.

POPEYE AND THE DANCING DUCKS

To hear a lot of people talk, you might think that the variety theatre ceased to exist once enough people had television sets and decided to stay at home in the evening.

Variety *did* go into a nosedive around the late Fifties and early Sixties, it's true. But not because television was so much better, as many writers and critics have assumed. What really happened was that greedy men were putting too many shows on the road, and after a while Joe Public said no thank you, I can find better things to do with my time and money, and stayed away.

It wasn't the best time to be starting out in the business. Some audiences, especially in the old music hall theatres, were never noted anyway for their patience, and when I made my début in 1959 at the Met in the Edgware Road the barrackers were well on their toes. After a particularly

poor joke from me, a voice from the gods bellowed:

'Get off!'

Another voice from the audience countered with: 'Give the kid a chance.'

Back came the voice from the gods: 'I'd give him eighteen months!'

A typical variety package in those days featured one hot star, maybe a singer with a hit record, surrounded by a load of rubbish. Audiences soon objected to having to sit around watching terrible acts for an hour and a half before their favourite came on. The rest was predictable. Profits turned into losses, and one after the other the old variety theatres closed, or were made over to some other kind of entertainment. At which point the press began to talk about the 'death of variety'.

In fact, variety did not die; it is very much alive and with us today. Only the shape has altered, and that is a theme I will return to later in this chapter. For now, I want to remember some of the wonderful acts from my early days in show business – some of which, for various reasons, were unique and unrepeatable.

Take Henry Vaddon. Henry was a hard man, with an act that only a country still reeling from two World Wars and a couple of Depressions could produce. At its climax he used to catch a spinning cartwheel on his head. To help him, he had a spiked helmet like the old German soldiers used to wear. He span the cartwheel, then launched it in the air and got himself underneath. You could always hear when Henry's act was coming to an end. First you'd hear the fizzing of the wheel as it went up in the air, followed by. . . 'Chrisssst!' as it landed on the spike.

Just where Henry got the idea from I shall never know, but over the years I did notice that his neck grew shorter, and shorter, and shorter.

Henry Vaddon was one of Nature's one-offs. Ventriloquists, on the other hand, are a separate breed. Although rarely seen together – who would go to a show consisting of nine ventriloquists? – they share strange attitudes, and all are devoted to their dummies. Some prefer not to show this openly, and will sling the dummy in the boot of the car and leave it to look after itself. Others treat theirs like a companion, or a child, and cannot do too much for it.

I worked with a vent called Eric Grenville, who undoubtedly came into the second category. His special friend was a man-sized Popeye doll which sat next to him on-stage while they chattered about Olive Oyl and spinach and other things dear to the heart of the sailorman. Off-stage, Popeye sat on a chair in the dressing-room, covered in a big sheet.

Also on the bill with me and Popeye was Johnny Hackett, a very funny Liverpool comedian. One evening before the show he and I were in the dressing room hanging up our suits. Eric Grenville had left Popeye on his chair and gone off for a beer in the bar. Johnny looked at the dummy and said:

'Let's have a laugh with Popeye. We'll put him on the toilet.'

Before I knew what was going on, I was helping Johnny drag this full-sized dummy down the corridor and into the toilet. On to the throne went Popeye, down came his trousers – he looked a treat, sat there with his wooden legs stuck out in front, trousers round his ankles, still puffing his pipe. We left him to it and shut the door.

Back in the dressing-room Eric Grenville arrived, frowned at the empty chair and asked us rather nervously: 'Have you seen Popeye, lads?'

'Well,' said Johnny, 'the last time I saw him he was going for a crap.'

Eric hurtled out the door and rushed to the toilet. Following at a safe distance, we saw him pull open the door and shout:

'Popeye! Popeye!' He disappeared inside and moments later we heard: 'Oh, Popeye, what have they *done* to you?'

Johnny and I were weeping with laughter as Popeye, his dress adjusted, was carried back to his proper place in the dressing-room. Frosty times followed; Eric would not speak to us for several days.

Hot shoe shuffle

I hope we can laugh about it now, but in those days I saw some speciality acts that would have had the animal rights people rubbing their eyes in disbelief. One feller went round the halls with a troupe of ducks which danced the Can-can. They lined up on top of a piano and, when the music started, they danced. They even sang the words:

'Quaaack quack-quack-quack-quack-quack-quack Quack-quack-quack-quack-quack-quack Quack-quack-quack-quack-qua-qua-qua-qua . . .'

You know how it goes. As the music went faster, so the ducks danced faster, really flinging their little feet up in the air. Audiences thought they were wonderful. The only thing was, they weren't really dancing at all. No. The feller, you see, had a hotplate on top of the piano. So, instead of all that 'Gay Paree' nonsense, what the ducks were really saying was more like: 'Ouch! Ooh! Jeez-us!'

How times have changed. This morning I read in my newspaper that a play has had to be rewritten because the original version was thought cruel to the goldfish which plays a leading part in the action. The play, it seems, is about a marriage which is breaking up and the goldfish is the trigger which sets the action going. As the paper reported:

'In an out-of-town run in Barnet, the fish in question was thrown out of the window. Although a bucket of water was provided for it to land in, the scene angered animal rights activists. Now the play has been rewritten to allow the fish to remain in its bowl throughout.'

I am delighted that serious dramatic parts, at last, are being written for goldfish. All the same, I can't help thinking that twenty years ago they wouldn't even have bothered with the bucket!

Whitewashing the Victoria Palace

Monsewer Eddie Gray of that wonderful, unique bunch, the Crazy Gang, had an act with pigeons. No hotplates or toasters – just a very funny act in which his little group of performing pigeons was made to seem uncontrollable. If he pointed to his right, the pigeon went left. If he pointed to the top of his head, the pigeon fluttered down and landed on his knee.

One day Bud Flanagan was coming back on the train from Brighton when he met Dickie Hurran, a famous and well-loved producer. They sat together for the rest of the journey and Dickie could not help noticing that Bud had a metal lunch-box on his knee. Bud offered no explanation, but before they got to London he did persuade Dickie to come to the second house that night.

'Yes,' he said, in his quiet reflective way, 'it should be rather interesting.'

So along went Dickie to the Victoria Palace, half-wondering if the Crazy Gang were going to pull some special stunt that night. All was reasonably normal until they came to Monsewer Eddie Gray's act with the pigeons. He came on with his usual wicker basket, released the catch and – Bang! Out flew a seagull which had been cooped up all day in the lunch box

– ever since a fisherman in Brighton, bribed by Flanagan, had caught it and stuck it in there.

Well, if you have ever been to the seaside you will know that seagulls are not small. They have big wings, and a body to match, and when the body has been closely confined all day. . . This seagull went beserk in the theatre. It flew everywhere; it crapped everywhere. Quite apart from the panic it caused, as it soared past people's noses (and whitewashed their toupees), that bird knocked up a bill for damages of more than two hundred quid – which in those days was a lot of damage.

That was one of the great nights at the Victoria Palace. On their own home patch in Victoria Street, the Crazy Gang were a law unto themselves. Away from it, they were still irrepressible. If you were on the same show with them, it was fatal to say that you had someone special coming to see you that night.

'Who is that?' they would want to know.

'Lord and Lady Farnsbarns, actually.'

'Oh. Really.'

After the show you would be entertaining these special guests in your dressing-room, when the door would open. In steps Eddie Gray, wearing a top hat but stark naked otherwise. He looks round:

'Oh,' he says, 'I'm so sorry. I didn't know you had company.'

That is just for openers. Then he walks over to your guests, shakes them all by the hand, says to each one: 'I'm *so* pleased to meet you' – and finally walks out through the open door, hiding nothing.

Very big with trombonists

This talk of buttocks, even those of Monsewer Eddie Gray, is enough to remind me that the old-time variety theatre could be a hotbed of passionate relationships. Like the shows performed in the theatres, these secret liaisons usually ran for a maximum of one week only, with as many performances as the partners could agree to – though sometimes they did not see eye to eye. As a young trampolinist confided to me, having spent a week in Portsmouth closeted with a nymphomaniac knife-thrower's assistant:

'Monday afternoon was great. So was Monday night. Tuesday was terrific. Wednesday, well . . . Wednesday wasn't bad, but on Thursday, Thursday was *very* demanding. On Friday, I can tell you, the demand was still there – but I had nothing left!'

Poor lad, he would have been better off with Debbie. She was a dancer – attractive, popular, a broad-minded girl with an eye for a good-looking feller. What she could never understand was why she always ended up with the trombonist. Every time she travelled to a new theatre – bingo! A new trombonist entered her life.

The answer lay in the band parts. As the music for Debbie's show was taken from theatre to theatre, so it fell into the hands of different resident musicians. At the first band-call in a new town, when the musicians and artistes ran through their music together, the trombonist opened his music for the chorus and there, written among the printed lines and dots, was a message. It read: 'The third one from the left is a bloody good lay.'

'Hmm. That's very nice of someone,' said the trombonist to himself, looking along the row and counting.

'Blimey!' thought Debbie, as their eyes met. 'It's happened again!'

Some relationships were more complicated. There is a story, treasured among people with their own memories of variety, about a pair of musical Siamese twins. They were identical in every detail, except that in their act one played the trumpet and the other the saxophone.

One week in Nottingham, the trumpet-playing twin found herself strongly attracted to the second top, a comedian. The comedian was keen, and asked her out for coffee, but first he wanted to know if it would be alright with her sister.

'Sure,' said the trumpeter. 'If one of us goes out for coffee with a guy, the other one reads a book.'

So they went out for coffee, and everything was fine. The next evening, the comedian wanted to take her out for supper after the show, but first he wanted to be quite sure it would be alright with her sister.

'Sure,' said the trumpeter. 'If one of us goes out at night with a guy, the other one writes letters and does the accounts.'

So they went out for supper, had a wonderful meal by candle-light, plus a couple of smoochy dances, and everything was fine. Afterwards, the comedian wanted to spend the night with his new girlfriend. She said yes, but saw him hesitate.

'What is it?' she asked him tenderly.

'Well,' he said, 'if I go to bed with you . . . I mean, are you sure it's alright with your sister?'

'Of course,' said the trumpet-playing twin. 'If one of us goes to bed with a guy, the other one practises her instrument.'

So they all got into bed, the comedian and the trumpeter made wonderful love together, and, just to one side, the other twin practised the saxophone for two hours.

Next day, the girls were standing by the stage door when the comedian came along – and walked straight past them without saying a word. The trumpet-playing twin burst into tears.

'Did you see that?' she sobbed. 'He didn't even look at me!'

'Never mind,' said her sister. 'Perhaps he didn't recognize you.'

Yes, those were the days. Days of wonderful fantasy when men like The Great Whappo strode the boards. His speciality was bending six-inch nails over his willy. I ran into him the other day; he is now seventy-five years old.

'Are you still doing the act?' I asked him.

'No,' he said. 'Me wrists have gorn.'

You won't find acts like that any more! But you will find others that are just as imaginative. To return to my earlier theme, about the changing shape of variety, things may not be quite as they were in show business, but the basic ingredients are still very much around.

Take the summer shows. They soldier on, and some do very well with a run of six weeks or so. Gone are the days of the twenty-two week run, but that is because the old British resorts are not what they were. Literally millions of people who would have spent a fortnight by the sea in England are doing the same thing in a warmer climate – in Spain, or Greece, or Italy. When I did my first season at Blackpool, on the North Pier in 1964, there were three pier shows – Central, South and North – the Ice Show, the Queen's, the Circus, the Winter Gardens, the Opera House, the ABC – that made nine major shows, plus a straight play at the Palace, and other live entertainment all over the town. Then I did a terrific summer season with Harry Secombe at the Palladium in *London Laughs,* which ran for nine months with three shows every Saturday. Luckily I was only twenty-four/twenty-five, with all the energy in the world and the strength of a bull. It showed, too – Secombe, a somewhat older man, was knackered!

Nowadays the emphasis is on shorter runs, because the public are more restless and want more entertainment. It suits the performers as well, because they want a more varied life instead of being stuck for months in one show. At the same time, there has been a thinning-out process, and the emphasis is now much more on *quality.* Many years ago, when I was in pantomime with Frankie Vaughan, he said to me:

'Surround yourself with talent.'

He was right then, and he is right now. It's something I have tried to do in my shows, like *Live From Her Majesty's* and *Tarby and Friends.* On both series I have been able to say who I have wanted with me, and I have been backed up 100 per cent by my producer David Bell and London Weekend Television. Always, when I go on the road, I want to know I am surrounded by very good performers. It pays off all round. Everyone in the show has a good time, and the audience come out saying: 'What a good night that was!' Twenty years ago there was a tendency for audiences to say: 'Well, he was alright, but the rest of it was terrible.'

Today, I like to think, standards are up and audiences more discriminating. There is still plenty of room for good, fresh speciality acts, and the Popeyes and performing pigeons need not go hungry, especially if the act works as well on television as it does in the theatre. Which reminds me of another maxim of show business – you cannot please all of the people all of the time.

As proof, I offer a moment from my own not-unspeckled career. We held a big benefit night in Liverpool for Ian Callaghan. Lots of big stars came and performed, people like Clodagh Rodgers, Dickie Henderson and Michael Parkinson were there. At the reception afterwards, a local feller came up to me and said:

'Hey, Tarbuck. You were great tonight.'

I said: 'Thank you very much.'

'And that feller Henderson,' he went on, 'he's got a lot of class.'

I said: 'Well, he's a very stylish performer.'

'Yeah. He was great tonight. I really enjoyed the two o'yer. Because, on television, yer both bloody crap!'

THE KENNY LYNCH STORY

Few men since Napoleon can have survived more campaigns than my good friend Kenny Lynch. Below and in later chapters I recall some of the more repeatable incidents from his life and times.

Singer, songwriter, comedian, golfer, footballer, tireless charity worker – Kenny is a man of many parts, and the Sunday newspapers want to know where he keeps his spares. He also has that great quality of not taking himself too seriously – of enjoying the moment. It is just as well that he has a good sense of humour, because while I would not say he was accident-prone, even he would not claim he was the best-organized man in show business. For example:

Kenny went down to Buckingham Palace to receive his OBE, awarded for his contributions to charity. He was in a high state of nerves, but that is nothing new on such occasions. (Even the cool and normally unflappable Bernie Winters, on being presented to the Queen at a Royal Command Performance, said: 'It's nice to meet you, Your Worship,' and spent the next half minute huffing: 'I didn't mean Your Worship, Your Majesty. I meant Your Majesty, Your Majesty.')

Kenny was shepherded into line by an equerry and given the drill. The Band of the Guards was playing in the gallery, and that day it was to be Her Majesty The Queen who was presenting the awards.

'When it is your turn, Mr Lynch,' said the equerry, 'you will take four paces to the right, turn left, step down two paces, turn left and you will be in front of Her Majesty.'

The great moment came, Kenny received his signal and off he marched. Four steps to the right, left turn, two steps down, turn left – and there she was.

'Whew,' thought Kenny with relief. 'Got that out the way.' He bowed, and another official murmured to Her Majesty that this was Kenny Lynch, the singer.

'Ah, yes,' said the Queen. She looked at Kenny and asked: 'And how long have you been doing it, Mr Lynch?'

In his nervousness, Kenny thought she was asking him: 'And how long have you been here, Mr Lynch?' So he said:

'I was born here.'

'Pardon?' said the Queen with a polite smile.

'I was born here,' repeated Kenny. 'I'm *from* here.'

'Oh,' said the Queen, 'well that's, um, very nice.'

Quite what she thought of him at that moment, we shall never know. Next thing, Kenny had collected his medal and was beginning to walk away, when suddenly he realized what the Queen had asked him. So he immediately turned back, gave the Queen a quick wave and tried to put the record straight:

'Oh, er, what I meant, er, I've been...'

But the next person was already in position; the way was blocked and the Queen did not see him. Kenny switched from one leg to the other, forward on his left, then back on his right as he fought to retrieve an impossible situation. At last his brain told him: 'Get out of here. Quick.' Which he did.

To his credit, Kenny tells this story brilliantly against himself, with every word and gesture, regal and otherwise.

Tarbuck on Showbiz

SUNDAY NIGHT AT THE LONDON PALLADIUM

My first time at the Mecca of entertainers was nearly my last. As I waited in the wings – the cheeky lad from Liverpool who five years earlier had been a complete unknown – I had a growing feeling that brown corduroy trousers and bicycle clips would be more appropriate gear than an evening suit. When Bruce Forsyth began to introduce me, I knew the meaning of panic and seriously wanted to run away.

After a lightning bout of mental wrestling I persuaded myself to give it a crack, and all went well, but for a few seconds it was a finely balanced choice between fame and oblivion. If I had given in to that part of myself that wanted to rush off and hide, my career would have been finished at the very point when I was within minutes of becoming an overnight success.

That is a measure of the London Palladium, and its greatness. It was the only theatre in Britain where this sudden leap to stardom could be made. Before me, it had happened to Bruce Forsyth, Norman Vaughan, Don Arrol, Engelbert Humperdinck, Val Doonican... Thankfully, I passed the test, and the most marvellous heady days followed – champagne all the way,

The Beatles and Me, a million laughs, the stuff of everyone's best memories.

Meanwhile, I was still learning my trade – how to ad-lib, get out of a fluff, manage an audience that would not laugh. It was ironic to be serving an apprenticeship at the Palladium, but that was how it turned out for me.

It must be every compere's nightmare that he will forget who is on next. If he cannot produce a name at the critical moment, he is in trouble. One night while I was compering *Sunday Night at the London Palladium,* it was coming up to top-of-the-bill time. I was out there on the stage, ready to make the introduction... and I went totally blank. I could *not* think who was coming on next. No name would come to mind, and there was nowhere to hide. I decided to brazen it out and said:

'Ladies and gentlemen, viewers. Someone who needs *absolutely* no introduction from me...'

And swept off-stage to bring on this very famous lady. After the show she said: 'That was the *nicest* introduction I have ever had in my life. Thank you.'

If she only knew the truth!

By the skin of my teeth I got out of that one, and learned a great deal from it. Other such moments would crop up later, but as you gain experience you try to find ways of turning a fluff to your advantage. You never get so relaxed that you lose your nervousness – you'd be slipping if you did – but you know there is no sense in paralyzing yourself with thoughts like: 'This is going out live to fifteen million people!' You don't need any reminders like that because it's hard enough to get through a show without making any blunders – roughly equal to a 6.0 for skating (on thin ice) plus a 10.0 for verbal gymnastics.

Nevertheless, if you have experience it gives you a reserve of options on which to draw in time of need. Recently, in *Live From Her Majesty's,* we had a boy from the *Dukes of Hazzard.* (Many fathers, like me, will know the show – it's the one where Daisy Duke, she of the beautiful bum, is always getting in and out of cars wearing hotpants.) The boy in question was John Schneider, who is also a talented singer. I introduced him like this:

'Now, ladies and gentlemen. Someone you all enjoy from Saturday evenings on television – from the *Dukes of Harris,* John Schneider!'

The whole audience roared with laughter. I thought: 'Oh, Christ', and walked off. There was nothing else I could have done. Live is

30

live, and you are stuck with what you have said. Unfortunately for John Schneider, he had to sing a slow patriotic ballad while the audience was still having a giggle about the 'Dukes of Harris'. When he had finished I was able to restore a little faith by saying:

'The Dukes of Harris! That is one of the Hazzards of live television.'

I wasn't completely off the hook yet. It became a talking-point the following week in pubs and offices throughout the land, so at the beginning of the next show I walked on and said:

'Here I am. The old Duke of Harris is back!'

The audience loved it. I don't think I would have handled it so neatly twenty years earlier, but in the course of those years I had arrived at a better understanding of audiences, and the almost mischievous pleasure they take from seeing a performer make a mistake – and then watching to see if, and how, he gets out of it.

Not that they understand everything, especially on the technical side. A feller said to me the other day:

'That show we saw last night, *Live From Her Majesty's*. When do you record that?'

'The day after you see it.'

'Really? How interesting.'

And off goes the punter, more than happy with his nugget of inside information.

So much for quick, responsive audiences. How about the totally silent ones? They are rare, but you do get them. I got mine not at the Palladium but at the Talk of the Town. When I came on, there was no greeting – what we call 'recognition applause'. It seemed odd at the time, but I had an act to do, so I gave them eight minutes of patter for not a single laugh, then stopped. I asked them:

'Do you know who I am?'

Peering round the audience I made out a few shrugs, a few mutters of 'No'. One or two more questions, and I was able to see what the basic problem was. As soon as I decently could, I got myself off-stage and started asking a few questions behind the scenes. One of them was: 'Why did no-one think of telling me we had six hundred Portuguese in tonight, and that none of them speaks a blind word of English?'

'Can you come back next week?'

For me, a lot of the magic of the Palladium came out of the Sunday night

show which I compered from 1965, taking over from Norman Vaughan. It was one of those very special shows which I don't think anyone around at the time will ever forget. The theme tune and that wonderful finale on the revolve – 'Dah-dah Di-da-di-dah-dah-daah-dah' – made you feel like royalty as you glided round in front of the audience. Mind you, I had to wait my turn. The first time I compered the show, the top-of-the-bill was Xavier

Cugat with his orchestra and Abbe Lane – and there wasn't room for everyone on the revolve. We had to stand at the front and do our regal waving from there.

And how about 'Beat the Clock'? That must rank as one of the grand-daddies of all today's game shows. I know Bruce has never forgotten it – whatever else he did later, people still remember him as the man who tore across the stage like a racing emu saying:

'Right, you've got £600, you've got £600. Can you come back next week?'

It carried over into his daily life. One day Bruce was working with a comedian we will call Billy Smith. Bruce came off-stage after rehearsals and walked into Billy's dressing-room to find him in a highly compromising position with one of the girls from the show. There they were, pressed against the wash-basin, both more than slightly pink in the face, clearly on the brink of a very private eruption. Billy turned his face towards the door.

'Right then, Bruce,' he said. 'Can you come back next week?'

Hong Kong in the cupboard

Wherever you work, you do better if you work with nice people. In the early part of my career, I was lucky to benefit from the kindness and helpful advice of some of the great stars of our business. Eric Morecambe has always occupied a special place in my esteem, and I have more to say about his genius in a later chapter – 'The Hardest Job in the World'. Just now I want to remember my first Royal Command Performance, in 1964.

I shared a dressing-room with Eric and Ernie, Tommy Cooper, and Dennis Spicer the ventriloquist. While Eric and Ernie were rehearsing, Tommy Cooper unplugged the phone and locked it in a cupboard. I was still very much the boy in those days, and may have looked a little bit surprised. Tommy gave his confidential cough, and explained:

'You've gotta watch these pros,' he said. 'While I'm on-stage, they'll be phoning Hong Kong.'

Then it was Tommy's turn to rehearse, and Eric and Ernie came back to the dressing-room. Eric was on to it in no time.

'Now then, Sunshine,' he said to me. 'Where's the phone?'

'Tommy's locked it in the cupboard. He said you'd be phoning Hong Kong.'

We had a laugh about it, then a few hours later we were all in the dressing-room, waiting for the Queen to arrive. Suddenly, just down the

corridor, the stage door telephone started ringing. Eric had the answer.

'Tommy,' he said. 'It's long-distance in the cupboard!'

That evening, I was in the second half of the show. The others had all been on, but I will never forget that Eric came down especially to wish me luck before I went out on the stage. It was typical of the man that he wanted to encourage a young fellow-comedian, and I have since tried to do the same for young people coming on my shows.

More than ever, I believe – to digress for a bit – people in show business need to work together, to learn from each other, to enjoy themselves and at the same time not be too serious about what they do. This wasn't how many performers saw things in the old days, when Variety bills were weighed down with prima donnas who thought it was necessary to be difficult in order to get respect. There are still some over-inflated egos in the business, however, and the petty rivalries and jealousies sometimes seem like an occupational hazard.

And yet I am convinced there is a better way, and that most people in show business are prepared to work towards it. Life is really too short to do anything else. Take it from Old Jim. As a comedian in my forties, I *know* I am right!

The moon and a donkey

Harry Secombe was another great positive force in my early years. We were at the Palladium together in *London Laughs,* and it turned out to be not just a great fun show but, for me, a great learning show. It would have been difficult *not* to learn, doing sketches with Harry night after night for all those weeks, and three times on Saturday. But we had a lot of fun, and Harry was always generous towards me, letting me get my laughs and being glad for me when things went well.

One tiny flaw in my armour in those days was that I was a terrible giggler. I am quite proud of the way I have controlled it since then, but in the mid-Sixties I could be set off very easily. In one of our sketches Harry came on dressed as Mr Pickwick with a coach and horses, and I followed on a motor-bike dressed in all the leather gear while the band played the Kinks' song, *Dedicated Follower of Fashion.*

One night Harry broke wind – to put it mildly. It is terrible when it happens to a performer, but this one was in a class of its own. We started to laugh, then Harry made matters worse by muttering to me out of the corner of his mouth:

'Quick, nurse, the screens. Ooooooh. Pooh pooh. Nurse!'

Once he saw I was out of control, Harry kept it up for the rest of the evening. Every time I was on with him, he'd have another go:

'Oh, oh. Nurse! Oh! there's another one, Jim...'

I was helpless. I don't know how I got through the show. Not everyone, however, was quite so enraptured by our performance. About four days later Harry got a letter. Its contents were, approximately, as follows:

'Dear Mr Secombe, I am a commercial traveller from Birmingham. Recently I came down to London, and spent a long day calling on clients in the East End where I saw several placards which announced 'London Laughs' at the London Palladium, starring Mr Harry Secombe with Mr Jimmy Tarbuck, Thora Hird, Freddie Frinton, Russ Conway, Anita Harris and others. Thinking this would make an enjoyable evening's entertainment,

35

I went to the theatre, paid my money and sat in the third row.

'Obviously the jokes passed out of the side of the mouth between Mr Secombe and Mr Tarbuck were funnier than the ones that came over the footlights to the audience. In fact, they seemed to enjoy the show more than the audience. I also noticed that Mr Secombe came on with a coach and horses, and Mr Tarbuck appeared riding a motor-bike. I suggest you both get in a rocket and piss off to the Moon.'

What's more, he signed his name and gave us his address – a true critic! Harry and I still laugh about it when we meet.

The first half of *London Laughs* closed with a big Cockney singalong, for which the cast dressed up as Pearly Kings and Queens, and Harry Secombe and Thora Hird came on in a donkey cart, pulled by a real donkey. Everyone stood on the revolve and round we went – a classic Palladium finale.

After a few days I got talking to the man who owned the donkey. I said I thought the donkey had been very well-behaved and he said:

'Yes. The thing with donkeys is, you shouldn't feed them before they go on the stage. If you do, they get excited and disgrace themselves.'

'Really?' I said.

'Oh, yes,' he said. 'Sweets are lethal.'

'How do you mean?' I asked.

'Well,' he said, 'if they have anything sweet, it goes right through them. As soon as they get on the stage and see the lights, the old juices go to work and they do a load.'

Next day I went out and bought a box of liquorice allsorts. When the donkey was led out of its stall and brought into the theatre, it was tethered for a while in the corridor. I waited until no-one was around and fed it the allsorts. It seemed to like them. During the Pearly scene, Thora Hird was seated directly in line with the donkey's jacksie. They had only been on-stage about half a minute when up went the donkey's tail and – Wallop!

Thora went: 'Oooh!' and turned her nose to one side.

The audience roared with laughter and so did the rest of the cast. Thora had the next dressing-room to me, and after the show she said:

'Wasn't it *awful,* that donkey doing its business like that?'

'Yes,' I said, 'it certainly was.'

So I kept going out and buying more boxes of liquorice allsorts. Each time it worked a treat, and the best bit was hearing Thora's voice, rising above the music:

'Oooh, Harry! It's doing it again!'

Harry and I were talking about it a few days later. He asked me what was happening to that poor old donkey.

I said: 'I don't know, someone must be giving it sweets,' and burst out laughing. I retired hastily to my dressing-room.

Minutes later there was a loud thumping on my door, which I had taken the precaution of locking. Enough was enough. The donkey went back on its sweet-free diet.

Two Italians

Consternation at the Palladium! The top-of-the-bill in the Sunday Night show had dropped out only hours before we were due to begin.

The programme executives rushed
about and came up with the name of
Tito Gobbi, the famous opera star, who
was living down in Sussex. He said yes,
he'd do the show, and sing *La Donna è Mobile.*
Unfortunately, he couldn't supply any music.
No matter, said the programme people, they
would get it from the ATV Music Library at Elstree.

I arrived at the theatre at midday, ready
to rehearse from about two o'clock. A stagehand
asked me who was the new top-of-the-bill.

'Tito Gobbi,' I said.

'Not that ————— Italian mouse
again?' he said, meaning Topo Gigio, who had been
on a few weeks before (and who is the subject
of our next story).

I put him right about that, then around
six o'clock Tito Gobbi came on to rehearse. Well, it
may be mischievous to say so, but I just wish he had done
the show there and then, without a bandcall. It would have
been hilarious.

Like all the best disasters, it began without
a hint of what was to follow. Tito Gobbi strode
out to the front – a most impressive man – the

orchestra played the brief introduction: 'Ping ping ping ping-pa-ping...' and he began to sing. After a few notes he was about to open out with his magnificent voice – but the orchestra suddenly switched into the tune of *I'm Just Wild About Harry!*

No-one had seen it coming – that was the greatest part. Watching thirty people run over the edge of a cliff together would not compare with the way this orchestra drove itselve into the trap. As for Tito Gobbi, his face was the most wonderful picture of shock-horror I have ever seen. A live audience would have loved it.

What had gone wrong? It took a couple of minutes to sort out, but then all was made clear. The ATV Music Library had sent the music for *La Donna è Mobile,* but not the right *Donna.* This particular batch was the music for the start of an old Harry Secombe Show!

'Ah!' everyone said later. 'No wonder.'

Our second Italian is the mouse. Topo Gigio. To my mind he was the most lifelike puppet of his day. He had three people to work him, one doing the head, another the arms or front legs, and another the back end.

On this particular day the programme people wanted to try a little experiment with the timing of the show. Instead of presenting it live at eight in the evening, they wanted to record it at seven, then just as the recorded show was finishing, they would start the tape off from the beginning for the television audience. As far as the viewers were concerned, there was no change in the timing, and anyone looking in the *TV Times* or their newspaper found the usual announcement: '8.00. Sunday Night at the London Palladium, presented by Jimmy Tarbuck'. Nothing strange about that.

Unfortunately, the message hadn't got through to one of Topo Gigio's operators. He thought he wouldn't be needed until some time after eight, so he was off in the pub having a drink when he should have been working his part of the little mouse.

Out front, I was chatting away to Topo Gigio who was crawling up my arm – but then got stuck because there was no-one to work the props. So I had to hold up a rope for it to walk along.

'There you are, Topo', I said.

'Oh, thank you, Jimmee', replied the mouse.

Meanwhile, in between our little bursts of dialogue, I could hear the two Italians behind the set, cursing and blinding at each other and at their absent friend – who then turned up and received a right rollicking from the other two. The air was thick with 'Madonnas' and 'Miserable Pigs'. It was wonderful. I only wish there was a way of filming these 'invisible' disasters – I know the bloodthirsty viewers would love them (see also 'Not All Right on the Night').

Our gallant lads, or, a debt repaid

Another great star who helped to make the Palladium a lucky place for me was Arthur Askey. When he played my mother in pantomime there, he had been a legend in my eyes since I was a kid at school. Each week for years he'd been on the front of *Radio Fun,* performing in his own cartoon strip. Arthur was both very funny and wonderful to work with. He told me many show business stories in our time together. Here are two of them.

One year he was in pantomime in London with a flat-chested principal boy. The management decided the lady needed filling out and she was sent down to Bermans, the theatrical outfitters, to get some falsies. She tried on several pairs before she found some that were wonderfully suited to her figure. Feeling rather pleased with herself, she went back to the theatre and waltzed onto the stage during rehearsals.

'Well,' she said to Arthur, 'what do you think?'

'Very nice, dear,' he replied, 'but you're wearing the leading man's arse.'

During the war Arthur was a huge radio star, and was constantly asked to do shows and make appearances to help out the forces. One day, while he was in a show in Blackpool, he had a call from the commanding officer of a military hospital near Preston.

'Would it be possible for you to come over and see some of the lads?' asked the CO.

'I will do better than that,' said Arthur, 'I'll bring the whole show.'

He got everyone – 'Stinker' Murdoch, who was starring with him, the jugglers, the dancers – they all went and gave a complete performance in amongst the beds in one of the hospital wards. Needless to say, the show was rapturously received by the lads. Afterwards, the CO took Arthur to one side and said to him:

'Mr Askey, I can't thank you enough for what you've done for these men.'

'Thank me?' replied Arthur. 'I can't thank *them* enough for what they've done – fighting for us.'

'Fighting?' said the CO. 'There must be some misunder-standing. These men haven't done any fighting. This is a VD clinic.'

Hurriedly, Arthur gathered the girls together and exited to Blackpool!

Over the rainbow

I have mentioned my belief that performers should help each other. From my own experience, no-one responded better to a few kind words and consideration than the wonderful Judy Garland. She was coming to the end of her career, and one night at the Talk of the Town she decided she could not appear and I was asked to stand in for her. An announcement was made to the audience:

'Ladies and gentlemen, we regret to inform you that Judy Garland will not appear.' (*Loud groans*) 'But in her place we have Mr Jimmy Tarbuck.' (*Double groans*)

I went on, and had done about forty minutes when she came on behind me. There was no time or need to reason why – suddenly there she was. I greeted her and she whispered: 'Don't leave me alone on the stage.' So I held her hand, and carried on holding it while she went ahead with her act.

Shortly after this, it was decided to put a on a special, unscheduled *Sunday Night at the London Palladium* with Judy Garland at the top of the bill. On the day of the show, she got it into her head that the orchestra should play her introductory music for three minutes – and then she would appear and do her act. Well, that is OK – maybe – in the theatre, but on live television it isn't exactly gripping because all the viewers would see for three minutes was the empty stage, while the orchestra played *Somewhere Over the Rainbow,* then went into the *Trolley* song, etc. However, she was adamant and held out for her three minutes.

Came the show itself, and it was almost time for her introductory music to begin. In the wings the management people were *fuming:*

'That cow won't go on,' they were saying.

'No,' I said, 'and nor would I if you spoke to me like that.'

I went up to her dressing-room, knocked on the door and went in.

'Hi, dear,' I said.

She looked at me and said: 'Here's the little man with a lot of class.'

'The audience is waiting for you,' I said. 'They are a good audience. Why don't I walk down with you. If you want me to, I'll come on-stage with you, I'll come on and hold your hand.'

'Thank you,' she said. She got up, and we went down the stairs together. On my way up to her dressing-room a couple of minutes earlier, I had put the word round the stagehands, and now they all turned out and greeted her as she went by:

'Nice to see you, Miss Garland.'

'Glad to have you back, Miss Garland.'

Although she was by then a very frail little lady, she walked out on that great Palladium stage and performed her act, and went down very well with the audience. As a kind of insurance, she wanted me beside her all the time, and I gladly stayed with her. Next day the mischievous press were on the phone.

'Was she drunk or was she on drugs?' they wanted to know.

'No, she wasn't,' I told them. 'That was how we rehearsed it, and that was how we always wanted to do it.'

It was Judy Garland's last major television appearance. A few weeks later she was dead. I will always treasure those appearances we made together.

THE KENNY LYNCH STORY

Tom Jones was back in England for the first time since conquering Las Vegas. A big spectacular was planned and the dress rehearsal was set up at a packed Elstree Studio with a forty-piece orchestra – the lot. Jonesy was due on to knock 'em dead with *Letter to Lucille*. I gave him the big build up:

'Ladies and Gentlemen, now for the young man who has just taken all America by storm – our very own Tom Jones.'

The curtains pulled back and the spot hit the centre of the stage. There was Lynchie with his trousers round his ankles, bent over with his backside pointing at the audience.

'Oh, gawd,' I thought, 'not at a dress rehearsal. That's really done it.'

From high in the control room came an instant instruction from the unflappable producer, Albert Locke:

'Make-up!'

THE HARDEST JOB IN THE WORLD...

... is to stand up in front of an audience and make them laugh. Audiences are never the same, and however much you may decide that this gag will get a bigger laugh than that one, you have no guarantee that your next audience will laugh at all. The fact is, the comic is the only performer on the bill whose act can be destroyed by the people he is trying to entertain. It can be a terrifying prospect, and the history of show business echoes with the moans of comics who couldn't take it any more.

For any comic, it's a long haul up to the point where his talent matures and audiences begin to accept that he knows what he is talking about, that he has a good understanding of life and people and can produce insights that are both believable and entertaining. By then he is usually about forty years of age, and in the previous twenty years has probably inflicted a great deal of pain and disappointment on audiences up and down the country. It doesn't bear thinking about. In any case, comedians are the last people who should stop and say sorry.

For the young comedian today, it's a very different challenge from the one I faced back in the late Fifties. In those days old-fashioned variety was beginning to crumble, but you still had regional comics who preferred to stay in their own territory – Scotland, the North, or London and the South – where they could tour for years with the same twelve minutes' worth of material. Nowadays the clubs which are the main venues for beginners need at least forty-five minutes. That is a lot of material, and because it's not easy to find that much, many youngsters tend to work too blue for my taste.

I am no prude, but I would never consider using half the gags these youngsters come out with, let alone the four-letter words. I won't deny that if it's done well, it can be hilarious – and someone like Billy Connolly has had me in stitches – but it's not the kind of material I would choose for myself.

Next, if he's any good, the youngster will be asked to do a summer season – there are still plenty of those about, and plenty of demand for touring or doing special one-night shows. By that time he may well have had his first taste of television, and he will have learned that it brings both good news and bad. The good news is that television pays well and gets his face and name before millions of viewers; the bad news is that he needs new material every time he goes on.

And that's just the beginning. Over the next twenty years he must patiently toil towards success and eventual stardom. If he gets that far, and can count himself among the ten or so top names in British comedy, he will reckon he's earned his rewards.

When I started out, I had the great good fortune to work with nice people. In that respect showbusiness is no different from any other walk of life – a little more glamorous, maybe, but in essence you still depend on the people around you to help you along and generally show you the way. The people who helped me were Harry Secombe, Eric Morecambe, Dickie Henderson, Max Bygraves, Frankie Vaughan, Mike and Bernie Winters. They all seemed to share the idea that one generation should find time to help the next, and that their business as a whole would benefit if they passed on their wisdom to people like me and answered my questions.

What did I want to know? Just about everything, but here

are one of two specific things that these people taught me. Dickie Henderson taught me how to take a bow. Frankie Vaughan taught me how to walk onstage, and do it with presence. Harry Secombe taught me all kinds of things – humility was one of them – and simply to work with him for nine months in *London Laughs* was a tremendously valuable experience for me.

Eric Morecambe was always generous. He took me aside one day and said: 'Young man, you have something. No-one can tell you what it is, but never ask: "Why me?"' In other words, be yourself and don't try to analyze what makes you funny; if you do, you can make a terrible hash of your life and career.

I have always had a special admiration for Eric. To me, comedians come in two categories: men who say funny things, like Bob Monkhouse, and men who are funny, like Russ Abbott and Tommy Cooper. Eric Morecambe was the only man I have seen who could do both. When Morecambe and Wise were at their peak, with Eddie Braben writing the scripts, they were magnificent. Eric had this genius for taking good material and turning it into something out of this world, and of course in Ernie Wise he had the ideal foil.

As a youngster, my own model comedian was Max Miller, the 'cheeky chappie'. He wore an amazing floral suit, and gave the audience a wonderful mixture of confidential patter, jokes and poems, some of which were tinged with blue – at least as far as the BBC was concerned – but nothing like the things you hear today.

He had a way of repeating himself. 'Now here's a funny thing,' he'd say. 'Now here *is* a funny thing.' Or: 'I do feel tired. Oh, I do feel tired. I feel so tired, I could have a lay-down.' (Looks around the audience with a mischievous glint in his eye) 'Would anyone…? No.' (He checks himself) 'I went into this cafe…' And off he would go in another direction. A marvellous sparkling performer.

It is strange, looking at the world of comedy, to see what an amazing cross-section of people they are. A surprising number are not the jolly entertainer type at all, but are really quite introverted. Tony Hancock, for instance, only truly came alive as the character 'Hancock'; in private life he was a tortured, unhappy man. Tommy Cooper, on the other hand, was the same off-stage as on; he didn't change. Max Bygraves has always been very laid-back about his work, whereas Bob Monkhouse works harder at it than any other comedian in history. He is the dedicated type, always immaculately prepared when he goes into the studio. Then you get the likes of me, the bad rehearser. I often don't know what I'm going to say until I'm actually walking on. This can frighten producers, but it's the way I am. The adrenalin doesn't flow for me in rehearsals, so I save my big effort for the moment I have to go out there and perform to a live audience.

For another contrast, take Norman Wisdom. A meticulous worker, he will rehearse and rehearse a sketch exactly as he's going to do it for real, and go on rehearsing it until he's got it just as he wants it. I'm not saying he's wrong to do this, but I know I couldn't work like that.

Another superb professional is the singer Billy Eckstine. We had him on *Tarby and Friends* not long ago and at 2.30 he arrived for rehearsals. Very laid-back, seventy years old but still very much the man's man – good golfer, good drinker, wonderful singer, and has been known to wink at a lady. Joe Cool. He came on the stage, met forty musicians for the first time, and sang that beautiful song *As Time Goes By* – the one I always call the Humphrey Bogart song. Perfect.

'Aah, Jim,' he said to me. 'I could have phoned this in.'

'That was great, Billy,' we said. 'See you tonight.'

No need for him to come to the dress rehearsal. We knew he'd be great on the night. Which, of course, he was.

Max Wall is another whose routines are planned in minute detail. Everything has its place, slotted in at a particular point in the act because he knows from long experience that this is where it works best. And silences. Long pauses while he peers out into the distance with an agonized look on his face – and no-one but he knows what is going to happen next. Because he has such control of his material, and facial expressions are an essential part of his act, he can tease out a silence so far that it becomes completely absurd and the audience responds by laughing.

There's certainly not much wrong with a comic who can get laughs for what he doesn't say, and I would also suggest that many of today's 'alternative' comics – the Shout and Charge brigade – would rapidly lose their bottle if they had to handle a script with silences built into it *à la* Wall.

For some while I have been watching this latest generation of comedians, and in some cases I have yet to see them do anything funny. I have seen Rik Mayall do funny things, and I know that my own children think *The Young Ones* is wonderful. I think it's all right, but too noisy for my liking. It's not necessary to shout and scream to get laughs, and I prefer the kind of comedy show where the laughs emerge through the central characters and the tensions between them. Shows like *Dad's Army,* where Arthur Lowe was magnificent – *and* surrounded by a wonderful bunch of other characters; *Porridge; Steptoe & Son; Rising Damp; Only Fools and Horses; Fawlty Towers.* It's quite a long list – fortunately – and these are just some of the names. Some are good shows, and some are great shows. Occasionally you come across a show which is so good it becomes immortal. For my money, they could put the *Phil Silvers Show* on every night of the week and I'd be the last to complain. What Sergeant Bilko and his friends managed to create in half an hour, other shows never get near in a whole series.

So, for beginners in the art of comedy the lesson is clear. If you want to learn, watch the best. Even if they are over eighty, like Bob Hope and George Burns, they don't lose their wonderful timing, their unrepeatable magic. Catch them while you can.

LEGLESS THEY SERVED

Robert Newton was a wonderful, wonderful actor. What is more, he and his great buddy Wilfred Lawson were two of the greatest drinkers the theatre has ever known. Judged by their performances on-stage, these men were first-class; judged by their performances with glass and bottle, they were out of this world.

They were appearing together in *Henry V* at one of the Shaftesbury Avenue theatres. Newton was playing Henry V and Wilfred Lawson was the Duke of York. One day the half-hour bell went for the 2.30 matinee. The assistant stage manager went round knocking on all the dressing-room doors. 'Half an hour, Mr So-and-so.' 'Right.' 'Half an hour, Mr So-and-so'. 'Thank you, duckie.' He knocked on Robert Newton's door. 'Half an hour, Mr Newton.' Not a sound. He went to Wilfred Lawson's dressing-room. Not a sound. Both men were missing.

Consternation in the theatre. Two of the leading actors had done a bunk, or at least had defied one of the cardinal rules of the theatre – that everyone should be present half an hour before the curtain. The producer had a fair idea that he would find them together in a pub – but which one? In the next ten minutes all the neighbouring pubs in Soho were scoured. The actors were found – but was it too late? They were not far from the theatre, but they were as drunk as skunks.

It was after 2.30 by the time the missing men had been helped back to their dressing-rooms. Instructions were given to hold the curtain a

Legless They Served

few minutes longer while the management went to work with black coffee and cold sponges. An announcement was made to the audience that, due to a technical fault, the performance could not start at the scheduled time; very sorry, etcetera. There was much impatient shuffling in the auditorium; programmes were rustled and read for the third or fourth time. Not until five to three did the curtain finally go up. At the start of Scene II, on came Robert Newton to a nice ripple of applause. He began:

'Where ish my gracious lord of, er... Prompt! Canterbury. Thank you. Where issh my grageous lord of Canbry?'

Duke of Exeter (briskly): 'Not here in presence.'

Silence, followed by King Henry: 'Oh. Me again, is it? Yes. Shend for him, good uncle.'

Earl of Westmoreland (with dread, sensing that a long afternoon lies ahead): 'Shall we call in the ambassador, my liege?'

King Henry: 'Not yet, my cousin. There are one or two... need to be resolved... before we hear about weight or shumming do wiv France...'

They battled on for about five minutes, but it was uphill all the way. There was a lot of nervous movement in the stalls, throat-clearing in the dress circle, and then, from the gods, up spoke a brave voice:

'Oi!' it said, loudly and distinctly. 'You're pissed!'

King Henry stared blearily into the lights, then tapped himself on the chest. 'Pissed, am I?' he said. 'Wait till you see the Duke of York.'

Wilfred Lawson was a legendary figure. One day in Soho he ran into another veteran actor. They got onto the sauce and reminisced about this and that. By around ten past two, they were extremely well refreshed, and Wilfred Lawson said to his friend:

'I know. We'll go down St Martin's Lane and have a look at a play I'm interested in. I'm sure you'll like it.'

Lawson led the way, they showed their passes at the door of the theatre and soon they were sitting in the circle with the matinee audience. Before the curtain went up, they discussed the play in tones that grew more and more slurred, and then the play began. After about ten minutes, Wilfred Lawson turned to his friend and said:

'Now, I wan' you watch thish scene very carefully.'

'Oh,' said his friend, 'and why is that, dear fellow?'

'Well,' said Wilfred Lawson. 'This is where I come on.

Should be mosh in'resting.'

He pursed his lips and squinted down at the stage, curious to see what happened next. A great man.

'Aye, Aye! That's yer lot!'

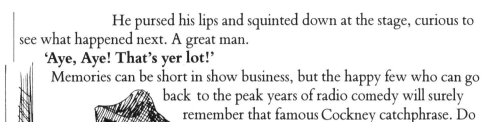

Memories can be short in show business, but the happy few who can go back to the peak years of radio comedy will surely remember that famous Cockney catchphrase. Do you remember him – always wore a hat, little moustache, carried a violin. Yes – Jimmy Wheeler – one of my all-time favourites. A wonderful stand-up music hall comedian.

Jimmy began his career working with his father, and the act was called Wheeler and Wilson. Old Man Wheeler was a large Edwardian figure; he carried a silver-topped cane and liked to speak grandly and a bit posh, even if he dropped a few aitches on the way.

In those days, as you also may, or may not, remember, people catching certain social diseases always went immediately to the nearest large public convenience to consult the notice board with the list of hospitals which could help them.

It so happened that young Jimmy had taken advantage of one of the cleaning ladies in the theatre where they had been rehearsing. A few days later it became painfully obvious that he had copped a dose of the deadly nervo and knox. His father – what a wonderful relationship! – took young Jimmy round to the hospital. The receptionist looked at the pair of them.

'Yes?' she asked.

'Ahem,' said Old Man Wheeler. 'We've come in answer to your advertisement at the Gentlemen's karzi in Leicester Square...'

Wonderful humour. Young Jimmy went on and built himself a great act. He had a way of speaking in short, confidential bursts – a wheezy, very music hall type of delivery with lots of emphasis on particular words. He would say:

'I had this *boil* on the end of my *nose*... I went to see the *doctor*...' (Leans forward) 'Well, I'm telling you... if you're going to have one, have a *big*'un... It was *throbbing*. I said: "Doctor. Look at this." "Well," he said. "You want to watch it." "*Watch it?*" I said. "I'm fed up with the bleeding *sight* of it!"

'Well, he took a *stick* out... It was only that long...' (Gestures) 'About eight inches... Well, he give it a *whack*... The vibration, I'm telling you, it tore the *tail off me shirt!*'

That was the Wheeler style. Magic. Another remarkable thing about him was the amount of drink he could swallow with no ill effects. There were times, of course, when it did affect him.

He had a daughter who lived in Paris. She had just had a baby, and Jimmy's wife had gone over there to look after her. He was doing a cabaret, and was due to follow her over to Paris on the last flight that night. He finished the cabaret and went straight to London Airport, dressed in his evening suit and carrying his violin.

He had had a few, but there he was anyway, checking in at London Airport. He went through to the departure lounge, and had one or two more. He heard the flight called for Paris Orly, so off he went, and got on the plane. As he told it:

'I was sat next to a *very* nice feller. He said to me: "Will you have a drink?" I said: "I *certainly* will." We had a few tipples together and I must have fallen *asleep.*

'Well, I woke up in *broad* daylight. Very hot. *Sunshine* streaming through the plane. I noticed, the feller next to me had *gone.* The steward came down the plane and I said to him: "Can I have a drink?" The feller said: "Certainly, sir." When he brought the drink, I said to him: "*What time* do we land at Orly?"

"Orly?" says the feller. "We're going to *Karachi.*"'

And they did. While his wife, daughter and son-in-law waited at Orly, Jimmy flew on to Karachi. He arrived in Paris three days later.

In about 1968 we had a midnight matinee in Great Yarmouth. It was a charity concert, and all the summer shows in town joined forces. There was Des O'Connor and his show, The Bachelors, myself and my show. Down the road at a small theatre Jimmy Wheeler was coming to the end of an immensely successful career. I said to the organizers: 'We've got to have him on the show.' He was a comic's comic – all the other comedians loved Jimmy. I approached him about it, and he said:

'*Thank you*, young man. What time do you want me?'

I said: 'Well, Mr Wheeler, it's a midnight matinee, so if you'd like to wander down there about quarter to twelve, we'll get you on about twenty past.'

'Suits me *fine*,' he said. 'Thank you very *much*, sir.'

He came down the pier on time – but legless. He'd had a skinful. I got him into a dressing-room, and gave him another one to keep him going.

'Thank you, son,' he said. 'You're a *toff*, the way you're looking after me.'

When it was his turn to go on, I introduced him and the band played his signature tune, *Let The Sun Be Your Umbrella.* Then, as he walked on, they continued playing. That was all part of the routine. He would say: 'Good evening', but be drowned by the band. As they carried on, he would shout: 'We've 'eard it! We've 'eard it! That's enough!' Then he'd do a few gags like: 'All right. It's not my *fault* you're not in the New Year's Honours List.'

That evening the Lord Mayor of Yarmouth was sat in the front of the stalls with all the local dignitaries and their ladies. Jimmy said:

'I was coming up the *pier* to do the show. I noticed there was a pile of *rice* by the entrance. I said: "Has there been a wedding?" A feller said: "No, we've just kicked shit out of a *Chinaman*.'

Well, there was uproar. People were on their feet, there were cries of 'Get him off!' Others were doubled up laughing behind their programmes. There was total hysteria for nearly ten minutes. Marvellous.

I will admit, there were times when Jimmy went too far. But it was a privilege to see him do it.

THE KENNY LYNCH STORY

My wife Pauline had a birthday party in Birmingham. Some years she is unlucky because her birthday, which is at the end of December, gets lost in the excitements of Christmas. This year, a friend called Eddie Futrell and his wife threw a wonderful party for Pauline. It was a great night. Kenny was there, the champagne flowed, and during the evening he acquired a young lady from among the guests. Later, when they got in Kenny's car together to drive back to his beautiful old cottage on the other side of Oxford, Kenny was well filled.

Dawn was breaking over the winding lanes of the Oxfordshire countryside as Kenny drove smartly round a corner and hit a milk float bang to rights. Bosh! He went straight up the back of it. In no time, milk was everywhere. The milkman, as it happened, was only yards away talking to the village bobby who was on his bike. There was no doubt about it. They had Kenny cold, and he was duly done for it. I let four or five days go by, then I phoned him.

'Mr Lynch?' I said, in a deep and serious voice.

'Yes,' said Kenny.

'McGregor here,' I said. 'Unigate Dairies.'

'Oh yes, Mr McGregor,' said Kenny, all warm and friendly.

I said: 'About our milk float...'

'Oh yes,' interrupted Kenny quickly. 'I'm gonna replace it. No problem. No problem. It's on my insurance, I can tell you...'

He was beginning to flap. I said: 'It's all very well you telling us that, Mr Lynch, but we are a milk float short at the moment, and we are having to deliver to that particular village by horse and cart. I am sure you will agree that in these difficult circumstances...'

'It's no problem,' Kenny almost shouted. 'I've been talking to my insurance company. It's all covered. No problem...'

I gave him a few minutes on the difficulties being endured in the offices of Unigate Dairies. I told him about the hardship to customers

56

and to the company, about how late the milk was arriving and how much it was costing to hire the horse and cart. Each time I paused, Kenny was in with more protests, assuring me that it was all under control, that the Dairy would get full compensation, etcetera. I let him have his say, then finally I said:

'Well, anyway, Mr Lynch, I am glad that you are treating this as a serious matter…'

'Oh yes. I am. I am,' came Kenny's voice, now good and agitated.

'Yes, indeed,' I said. 'Because, you know, it's no use crying over spilt milk.' And I started roaring with laughter.

When he could make himself heard, Kenny shouted back: 'Well, you can piss off as soon as you like!' And put the phone down.

As always, whenever I catch him and he has a chance to think about it, the next time we meet he comes out with the classic: 'I knew it was you.'

Did he ever. He had no idea at all.

WHO'S YOUR AGENT?

Every performer needs an agent – to look after him, get him good bookings and, he hopes, make him rich. In return for these services, the agent pockets a modest commission, enough to keep the wolf from his door – or so he says. Not that you see a lot of wolves hanging around agents' doors. In fact, most agents do very nicely – which is why performers spread envious rumours about them, for instance: 'Things in show business are so bad, my agent's eating bacon.'

Agents must be caring, interested people, always alert for an opening. Lew Grade thought he saw one back in the days when he was an agent. He went backstage after seeing an act and found the performer in his dressing room.

'You were marvellous,' he cried. 'Great. I've gotta have you on my books. Listen, who's your agent?'

'You are, Mr Grade.'

This was at a time when variety was still big business and the number of acts in circulation was a lot larger than it is today. The Grade brothers – Lew and Leslie Grade, and Bernard Delfont who formed his own company – were highly successful and became the most powerful agents in British show business. Neither surname is real, by the way. The family name is Winogradsky, but even old Mrs Winogradsky didn't stand on ceremony. She used to take holidays at various resorts where her sons had shows – two weeks in Bournemouth, a week in Blackpool, a week in Torquay. In Bournemouth and Blackpool, where the Grade shows were playing, she called herself Mrs Grade – but in Torquay, where it was a Delfont show, she was Mrs Delfont. And wasn't she well looked after!

Agents must always have impeccable taste, able to fit the right show to the right theatre and attract the right kind of audience. Some years ago an agency was booking theatres for a show called *Nights in Vienna*. In the office someone remembered that the Hippodrome in Birmingham was free, so they rang Val Parnell, whose theatre it was, and asked:

'How would *Nights in Vienna* go in Birmingham?'

Parnell replied: 'The same as *Nights in Birmingham* would go in Vienna!'

Agents, like Boy Scouts, must be truthful at all times, though their consistency has been questioned. A feller went into an agent's office one day.

'Who are you?' asked the agent.

'I'm a comedian,' he said.

'Prove it,' said the agent. 'Tell me a joke.'

The feller told him a joke. 'There you are,' he said. 'And who are you?'

'I'm Hymie Books the agent.'

'Prove it,' said the comedian. 'Tell me a lie!'

All this and ten per cent

Agents are often deadly with women. But this is all right so long as they are good at their job. A comedian came home one night to find his wife in tears.

'What's happened?'

'You won't believe it,' she said. 'Your agent came round this afternoon. He dragged me upstairs to the bedroom and raped me! He was horrible. He did vile things to me.'

'Oh, no,' said the comedian. 'That's terrible. Diabolical! Tell me, did he leave a message about booking me in pantomime?'

American agents are even smoother. At a dinner party one evening, an agent was struck by a beautiful woman sitting at the other end of the table. During the course of the meal their eyes met several times and she smiled at him. After dinner he went down to the other end of the table.

'Hello,' he said, 'I've admired you all evening.'

'Why, thank you,' she replied. 'Would you like to come into the garden?'

'Wonderful,' said the agent.

Then he noticed that the woman was in a wheelchair.

'That's all right,' she said, seeing him hesitate. 'Just wheel me out to the terrace.'

'You know,' said the agent when they were alone beneath the moonlight, 'I'm very attracted to you.'

'And I am to you,' answered the woman, looking up at him.

'Well, er, is there something we can do about it?' he asked.

'Yes,' she said, 'there is. Down at the end of the garden there's a beautiful old tree. On it there's a hook. Take me down there and I'll show you.'

The agent did as she suggested and soon they found the hook which was fixed to a sturdy low branch.

'I am wearing a special harness,' said the woman. 'At the back of my dress you will find a ring. Just slip that over the hook on the tree and we'll make love.'

He followed her instructions, and they made wonderful love.

'That was really great,' said the agent afterwards, as he helped the woman back into her chair.

'Yes,' she smiled, looking up at him. 'You know something?'

'What's that?'

'You must be from the William Morris Agency.'

The agent couldn't conceal his surprise. 'Yes. I am. But how did you know that?'

'Well,' replied the beautiful woman, 'those bastards from MAM always leave me hanging on the tree.'

Where do agents come from?

When they start out in the business, agents can either take the plunge on their own or join an established company as a junior. My manager, Peter Prichard, began his career with the Grade brothers, Lew and Leslie. At first he made himself useful round the office, taking messages and buying Lew Grade's cigars. Then he was given some bookings to arrange.

It was the age of the static nude, or *poseuse*. Shows featuring nude models were very popular on the variety circuit, but the law at the time made it an offence for the girls to move unless they were behind a curtain, so they used to appear in fixed, so-called 'artistic' *tableaux*. One morning Peter's boss came off the phone and said:

'One of the posers had gone sick in South Wales. You'd better find a new one.'

Peter went down to the Express Dairy in Charing Cross Road, which was the chief meeting-place for agents and variety performers. As usual it was full of artistes sitting around waiting for work. He noticed the comedian Hal Monty at one of the tables and went up to him.

'Oh, Mr Monty, I'm looking for a poser. Are any of these girls in here any good?'

'Wait a minute,' said Hal Monty, looking round. 'I know one.'

He called a girl over. 'Do you want a job tonight?'

'Yeah. All right.'

'This lad here can fix you up for a show in South Wales.'

Peter looked at the girl. She was pretty enough. He knew he should make sure she had good legs. It embarrassed him to ask, but he did so and she showed him. Fine. He sent her down to South Wales to do the show, and returned to the office feeling well pleased with himself.

Next morning there was hell to pay. The management in South Wales were furious. The replacement poser had been a disaster. She must have been wearing falsies in the Express Dairy, because by the time she reached the venue her breasts were many sizes smaller than they had appeared beneath her sweater. Yes, Peter should have asked to see them as well, but he hadn't liked to. In a Dairy?

Things were rocky for a while but Peter survived this setback and eventually thought his position in the agency was secure enough to try asking for a raise. He approached Leslie Grade.

'Yes, yes. I'll have a word with Lew.'

For a fortnight nothing happened. So he asked again.

'Yes, yes. I'll have a word with Lew.'

At last a meeting was fixed, and Peter faced Lew Grade across his desk.

'What's this you've been saying?' asked Lew, as if he had been offended behind his back. 'What is it you want?'

'I've been asking for a raise in salary, Mr Grade.'

Lew Grade's eyes narrowed. 'So how much do you think you're worth?'

Peter had to think quickly. He had no idea what sum of money to name, but he knew he'd be as good as dead if he failed to come up with an answer. Struck by a flash of inspiration, he said:

'I think I'm worth more than those cigars you smoke.'

Lew Grade's eyes opened wide for a moment, then the shutters came down again. He said:

'The day you give me as much satisfaction as I get from those cigars, you can have your raise. Until then, get out!'

For the time being Peter was defeated, and the subject of raises was not mentioned. Then one day, in the club they all frequented, Peter was just about to start a game of snooker when Lew Grade walked in. He called him over.

'What was that we were talking about in my office the other day?'

'Oh! About my raise, Mr Grade.'

'Yes. Well, you can have it – if you beat him.'

Lew Grade pointed a chubby finger at Peter's snooker opponent, who was a partner in another agency.

'That's just great, Lew,' called the opponent, who had heard this conversation. 'So how do you think I'm going to feel if I win and he doesn't get his raise?' Like a true gentleman, he lost – which made it a double victory for the Grade agency. Peter got his raise, and Lew Grade put one over on a rival!

In the Fifties the other way a young agent could get started was to rent his own office. Failing that, he could hustle in the Express Dairy, using the phone-box there as his office. That's what a certain young agent did for many months. Then one day as winter was drawing in, another agent saw him in the road in the pouring rain, struggling along with his date book under his arm, trying to find an act he wanted to book. He looked utterly miserable.

'Listen,' said the other agent, 'you can't go on doing this for ever. You've got to have an office.'

'I do okay,' said the first guy defensively. He looked up at the sky and pulled at his coat collar. 'Offices ... they're only a warm dry room with a desk and a telephone.'

The other agent took pity on him. 'Look,' he said, 'I'll tell you what I'll do. At my office we've got a very large cellar. We used to keep the coal in it, but we've just gone over to oil-fired central heating and we don't need the cellar any more. If you want to clean it out, you can certainly use it as an office. At least you'd be dry.'

So the feller agreed. He went in, cleared out the place, whitewashed the walls and fixed up a ceiling light. He bought a desk and two chairs in a second-hand office furniture shop, and in his attic at home he found a piece of old carpet and laid it on the cellar floor. 'Not at all bad,' he thought, looking round. 'In fact, bloody marvellous!'

He got some of his acts to come and see him. 'Look at this,' he said, waving his arms. 'Now I've really got an operation.'

Everyone was sitting (or standing) around admiring the view. There was a strange noise overhead. They looked up. The grating opened and an avalanche of coal came crashing into the cellar.

It was all a terrible mistake – the delivery should have gone to the cellar next-door. But try telling that to an agent.

True class

The London agent went to Hollywood where his client was making a pirate film with Twentieth Century Fox. When he arrived the agent was looking at his most prosperous – black silk suit, white tie on white shirt, all beautifully pressed. His client met him and introduced him to the movie executives, and they went to the Commissary for lunch.

'I'm doing well here,' thought the London agent as he looked round at the glamorous scene in the restaurant. Just beside him he heard his client building him up to one of the movie executives, and doing it well from what he could overhear in the hubbub. Something else he failed to quite hear was the water-jug as it caught his neighbour's elbow and two pints or more of tingling iced water shot into his lap.

The 'big' London agent stood up, the greater part of his dignity washed away in the deluge. People gathered round and were very sympathetic. He was led outside, each step he took marked by a small puddle of water.

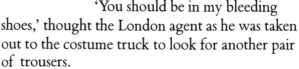

'This is terrible,' said one of the movie executives, 'but it should be no problem.'

'You should be in my bleeding shoes,' thought the London agent as he was taken out to the costume truck to look for another pair of trousers.

When they returned to the restaurant ten minutes later the 'big' London agent's loss of dignity was complete. The only replacement they could find was a pair of the tights worn by one of the pirates in the film. As he fondly remembers:

'I arrived in the restaurant the first time looking like the Godfather. I went back there looking like Max Wall!'

Agents are always right

An agent was devastated when one of his most important stars suddenly announced that he wasn't happy with the way his career was developing – and it was time they parted.

'But I've done so well for you in the past,' said the agent, spreading his arms wide. 'Why don't you give it another year. Stay on for another year and we'll look at it then, I promise.'

But the star was adamant. 'No,' he said, 'I'm leaving today. It's over. I'm signing with Harry Foster.'

'Please don't go,' the agent implored.

'Look,' said the star, 'it's fixed. I'm definitely leaving.'

'All right,' said the agent, but I'll tell you one thing.' He started to point with his finger. 'You walk out that door, and I guarantee you'll be back.'

'I definitely will not,' said the star. 'I've quit. I've left this office and that's the end of it.'

'I'm telling you,' the agent almost shouted. 'Walk out that door now, and you'll be back.'

The star pulled a face. 'Listen. I'm not arguing any more. I'm going.'

He marched out of the office and slammed the door. About five minutes later the door opened more slowly, and in came the star. He looked a little sheepish but, without saying anything to the agent, walked across the office to the hatstand, picked up the raincoat he'd left there and headed for the door again. The agent could not conceal his feeling of triumph.

'You *see*, Charlie,' he cried. 'I told you you'd be back.'

These three fellers ...

Wherever professional people meet, the deeds of show-business agents are legendary. One classic encounter happened in a bar, where a lawyer, an architect and a show-business agent were having a drink together. Each man had his dog with him.

The lawyer said: 'You know, this dog of mine is the most brilliant dog I have ever seen.'

The architect said: 'Hold on a minute. I have to tell you that my dog is *brilliant*. Yours may be brilliant, but this one here is *brilliant*.'

The show-business agent said: 'If you only knew. I have been in the theatre business for twenty-five years and I have seen some brilliant dogs but I assure you that this dog here is the best ever. He is brilliant plus!'

There was only one thing to do: put the dogs to the test. The lawyer's dog went first. The lawyer gave it a piece of paper and a pen, and the dog immediately wrote out an invoice for £50,000 plus VAT and dropped it at the feet of his master.

'Isn't that incredible?' asked the lawyer. 'That is truly the most brilliant dog I have ever seen.'

The architect said: 'Hold on. Wait till you see this.' He called to his dog: 'Wren!' and threw it a box of matches. The dog shook the matches out on the floor, and built a replica of St Paul's Cathedral with them.

'Isn't that wonderful?' demanded the architect. 'Have you ever seen anything as good as that?'

'All right,' said the show business agent. 'Now it's our turn. Risko!'

The agent's dog stepped forward. Eyeing the other two dogs carefully, it lined them up, mounted each in turn, took a gin and tonic from its master, drank it, had another and then strolled out the door.

The lawyer and the architect watched with open mouths. 'Where's he going now?' they asked.

The agent replied: 'When he's had a few at lunch, he usually takes the afternoon off and plays golf!'

THE KENNY LYNCH STORY

Lynchie is an ebullient character. He will talk to anybody. He is almost American in the way he goes round saying: 'Hi! Hello, Bob. Frank, nice to see you. Phil!' A lot of people like this quality in him because they think: 'How nice. How nice of him to have remembered our names.'

Of course, he can't remember them at all. At such times he needs help and advice from his friends. One night in Tramps he saw a face approaching and whispered to me out of the corner of his mouth:

'Who's this feller coming in?'

'That's Peter Griffiths,' I said.

'Of course it is,' said Kenny, and moved out to greet him. 'Hello, Peter. How are you?'

The feller said: 'My name is John Sanders.'

'John!' cried Kenny. 'Of course. How are you, John?'

Kenny turned back to me, and I thought I heard him mutter something like: 'Y'arsted.'

NOT ALL RIGHT ON THE NIGHT

Disasters in the theatre have at least one thing in common: somebody always gets a laugh, and usually it's not the performer who is suddenly the centre of attraction. He has his laugh later, when he gets out of hospital! That's not to say that every disaster is accompanied by violence and/or injury to the person; sometimes the pain goes no further than extreme embarrassment.

Hugh Lloyd was not so fortunate. He and I were appearing at Wimbledon in *Jack and the Beanstalk,* and Hugh had just come back to work after a week off with a bad dose of 'flu. He was maybe feeling a bit groggy, but outwardly he seemed OK and raring to be back in action.

He used to come on early in the pantomime and get the audience warmed up with an old music-hall favourite, *Hello! Hello! Who's your lady friend?* I was still putting on my make-up in the dressing-room, and not due on for another twenty minutes, when Hugh made his entrance.

There is a steep rake to the stage at Wimbledon, and Hugh came flying on, full of bounce. 'Hello!' he cried to the audience, 'Hello!' and dashed down the rake towards them. 'Who's your la-...'

69

He never finished the line. He was going so fast, he went clean over the footlights and into the pit. The audience let out a huge roar of laughter – and then went deathly silent when they realized that Hugh's dive was not even slightly rehearsed. Up in my dressing room I heard the roar and thought: 'Hello. Has he put in something new?' Then I heard the sound of running footsteps, followed by 'Knock-knock-knock' on the door and a voice shouting: 'Mr Tarbuck! Mr Tarbuck! Mr Lloyd's in the pit!'

So there was I, still in my underpants, urgently needed on-stage to keep the show going. As quick as I could, I pulled on my trousers and got down to the wings where there was high confusion. Chaos everywhere. Hugh was obviously hurt, and being carried out of the pit, and no-one could decide what to do next. We had to close the curtains and re-start the pantomime. Poor old Hugh was off work for another ten days!

A more modest disaster occurred one day at the National Theatre complex, where at one time they had three theatres – the Cottesloe (now closed), the Lyttelton and the Olivier. From the outside the whole thing looked, and still does look, like part of Hitler's Atlantic Wall, while inside, especially where the performers have to go, it is a maze of passages and very very easy to get lost there.

Albert Finney was starring in *Othello* and Beryl Reid was in another play in a neighbouring theatre. Beryl had been out to do some lunchtime shopping. She came back to the theatre, and set off along one of the passageways, turned a few corners... and found herself on-stage during a performance of *Othello*.

Albert Finney was in mid-speech when this familiar-looking lady carrying a shopping bag came across the stage towards him and suddenly stopped. And stared.

'Oh! I'm terribly sorry, Albert,' said Beryl. 'I've come in the wrong place.' And walked straight off again.

On another evening of contrasts, Sir John Gielgud was appearing in a quiet conversation piece while next door they were re-enacting the Russian Revolution. Gielgud was on-stage, holding an earnest dialogue with a fellow actor before a packed house of all those old ladies who love him when – suddenly, deafeningly, over the amplifiers in *their* theatre came the Russian Revolution.

Everyone in the place went twitchy while all around them boomed the noise of the storming of the Winter Palace. No-one could hear a thing. Gielgud looked particularly upset, and beckoned to one of his fellow

actors who crossed the stage to talk to him. Just as he got there, the
electricians regained control and the Russian Revolution was switched off.
Too late, unfortunately, for Sir John who was left roaring:

'What the ———'s going on?'

This was greeted by horrified gasps, then silence. 'Oh,' said
Sir John, stepping forward quite unconcerned and peering out at his
audience. 'I'm so sorry.' And went straight back into the play as if they had
never been disturbed.

Mule tray

When I was very young I was a guest star along with Jimmy James in a show
called *Nights at the Comedy* at the Comedy Theatre in London. This was
where I first came into contact with Mr T. Steele and his jokes. One night he
very kindly offered to drop me off at the theatre.

I got in the car with him and a boy called Frank Manzi, and

we headed for Picadilly Circus. That was as far as we got, because they decided to drive round and round the Circus instead of taking me to the theatre which is in Panton Street, off the bottom of Leicester Square.

'Listen, fellers,' I said, 'I'm going to be late if you don't take me down to the theatre.'

'No, no, Jim, you'll be alright,' said Tommy. 'Plenty of time.' He grinned at Frank and round we went a couple more times, leaving me stewing in my seat.

'Look,' I said, 'I haven't got time for this. Will you just pull over and stop and I'll walk there.'

'That's okay,' said Tommy. 'You've got hours yet.' And he flashed the famous teeth at me. Round and round the Circus we went, until a young Liverpool comic cracked and in a moment of panic leapt from the moving car into the whirlpool of the evening traffic and ran all the way to the theatre.

One evening I was in my dressing room when there was a knock on the door and a feller came in.

'Hello, Jim,' he said. 'Nice to be working with you. I'm Bob Tray.'

I said: 'Oh, hello, Bob.' I'd never met the man before, but he wanted to tell me something.

He said: 'I'm glad you've got away on the telly and become successful. I wonder if you'd watch my act and give me a few hints on timing. Yours is so good, I'm sure I could learn from you.'

This was very agreeable to my ears. I had never seen Bob's act but assumed he was a comedian. I said: 'Yes. Sure. Be a pleasure.'

He went away, and maybe half an hour went by, then he was back. He said: 'Jim, I'm on in five minutes. You will watch, won't you?'

'Yes,' I said. 'Sure.'

I went into the wings to watch, and the band started playing *Mule Train.* Then Bob started singing: 'Mule trai-in ... clippety-cloppin' over hills an' plain..'. In his hand was a tin tray. He reached the line 'Seems as though they're gonna – Bash!'

He gave himself a great crack over the head with the tray. And kept on doing it. Each time in the song you usually hear the crack of the mule driver's whip, he bashed himself with the tray.

I went into hysterics. The audience loved it, and he brought the house down with just this one number. Bob was delighted with his success, and one night, with the exuberance of it all, he got a little bit carried away.

In front of the stage was a short flight of stairs running down to the front row. Bob was well into his song – 'Mule trai-inn... Whack!' – when suddenly he ran down the stairs and cracked this feller in the audience on the head with his tray! The feller jumped up from his seat and gave Bob one straight back – right on the chin – and knocked him spark out!

Poor old Bob. That song with the tray was his one claim to fame. A delightful man.

'It's not un-us-ual...'

In my stage act I used to do a Tom Jones impression. I'd sing a Tom Jones hit and go into a microphone-swinging routine. One night in Nottingham I started swinging the microphone and it suddenly came off the lead and went flying into the audience like an Exocet missile. Amazingly, a feller in the fourth row reached up and grabbed it out of the air. But it could so easily have been a real disaster, because a mike travelling level with the ground at that speed could have caused serious damage if it had hit someone, maybe knocking out an eye or even killing them.

I thanked the feller who caught it, and got a lot of mileage out of the incident during the rest of that evening's show. But it shook me, and I said to my musical director, Johnny Wiltshire:

'Cut the Tom Jones out. I'm not going to risk that anymore.'

Appearing on the bill with me was Bernie Clifton, a big 'prop' comic and a very funny man. The next evening I got to the theatre nice and early, and the show began. I wasn't due on until the second half, but soon we were coming up to the interval. Then the Stage Door sent a message over the tannoy saying I was wanted on the telephone.

I picked the phone up but there was no-one on the other end. I waited for a bit, then I waited a bit longer. Now it was the interval and I was due to be getting ready to do my act. In the end I had to put the phone down and leave it.

I got the make-up on quickly, and the suit, and then it was time for me to go on. About twenty minutes into my act, where I usually did the Tom Jones bit, the band suddenly started playing the intro music for *It's Not Unusual*. I looked down at Johnny Wiltshire.

'No,' I said to him. 'I'm not doing that.'

Too late. The band were blowing and I couldn't get out of it. So I started swinging the mike, and glaring at Johnny and giving him the 'You berk' look. Suddenly the house lights went on – something that was no

74

part of the act. Out there before me in the front stalls was the most amazing sight.

Earlier that day, Bernie Clifton had been out to a building site and he'd got hold of about two hundred hard hats. While they had me upstairs hanging on the phone, he'd given these hats round to all the people in the front part of the stalls and told them what to do. They kept the hats under the seats, and then as soon as the band went into the Tom Jones number they whipped them onto their heads.

As I looked down at them I was completely stunned. Row upon row of people in hard hats grinning up at me. Then they started laughing and soon the place was in uproar. It was the greatest practical joke that's ever been played on me. And it all came out of a near-disaster. *That,* if you like, is show business.

THE KENNY LYNCH STORY

Kenny and I were playing a week in Swansea. After one of the shows a feller asked if I would come on the local radio and do a morning phone-in show. I said yes, and spent a very enjoyable morning listening to records and chatting with the disc jockey and all the housewives of Swansea and the surrounding area who came through on the phone. We talked about them and their day, about show business and anything they wanted to ask. When I came off the air, the producer asked me if I thought Mr Lynch might like to come on the show.

'Sure,' I said. 'I'll tell him.'

'Can we expect him on Wednesday morning, then?'

'Yes,' I said. 'No problem.'

That evening at the theatre I told Kenny and he said: 'Fine.'

Wednesday morning arrived. Kenny went along to the studio

and I was sitting up in bed with a cup of tea listening to the radio when he came on the air. Knowing the routine of the show, I waited a bit and then phoned in. Using a medium-to-heavy Welsh accent, I said:

'I would like to speak to Kenny Lynch, please.'

'Who is that speaking?' asked the feller on the switchboard.

'Dai Evans.'

'Where are you from, Dai?'

'The Valleys.'

I was put through. On came Kenny.

'Ello Mr Evans,' he chirped.

'Were you in Porthcawl about two years ago?' I asked, knowing full well that he had been.

'Yes,' said Kenny brightly. 'I was there with Jimmy Tarbuck. We had a wonderful time. Great place, Porthcawl.'

'Yes,' I said, in a sombre tone. 'You met my daughter.'

There was a pause. Kenny went quiet. Remember, this was live radio.

'I met lots of people,' he said suddenly. His voice had changed; now he was wary and defensive. 'I met lots of people. We were in Porthcawl. It's a... People were very friendly towards us... You can ask...'

He was starting to blather, so I interrupted him: 'Look. Be a man. Pop round and see 'er and the baby.'

There was instant panic in the studio. By now I had my head in the pillow and was crying with laughter, totally unable to speak. Kenny, though, heard something familiar through the spluttering at my end. He shouted:

'That's Tarbuck! Taaaarbuck!'

The balloon went up. Chaos. When the hysteria died down, and I was able to speak, I pulled him up on something else he had said on the show. Earlier, he had been talking about his boxing days in the Army.

'What?' I said. 'Box? You couldn't box kippers. Good morning.'

I put the phone down. That evening at the theatre, Kenny was on-stage and, when I was due on, he said to the audience:

'Ladies and gentlemen. Will you welcome... from the Valleys... Dai Evans!'

The word must have gone round with hurricane force. The audience roared.

AFTERNOON MEN

In the old days of variety it was a problem to decide what to do with the long hours before the evening show. When he was on tour, which was often, the natural homes of the male variety artiste were the pub, the snooker hall and the racetrack. Each town would also offer free membership of the Conservative or Labour Club, and free passes to the cinemas and any other theatre in the area. Lady theatricals tended to favour the cinema.

Then came golf. Since the Sixties, it has been extraordinary to see just how many show-business people have happily succumbed to the disease. Quite apart from the fact that they can have an enjoyable few hours in the open air whenever they want, they can also earn a great deal of money for charity by giving a few hours of their time and turning up at a Pro-Celeb match, or a Celeb-Am, or whatever. This is very rewarding for an entertainer, because he knows that after he's finished playing, some handicapped child or disabled person will benefit from the funds that he has helped to raise.

Sometimes we just play for fun. I went to play at a very exclusive golf club with Engelbert Humperdinck. He arrived in a great Rolls

Royce, bigger than a block of flats, with the black windows and the EH numberplate. He lifted his golf bag out of the boot. It was white, with 'ENGELBERT' printed in big letters down the front of it. He wore black glasses and an elegant cashmere sweater.

He said to me: 'Jim. You go in and do the green fees, will you. I don't want anyone to know I'm here.'

There are many stalwarts of the charity golf scene, but perhaps one of the most active is Henry Cooper, a wonderful charity worker who has raised money for all sorts of organizations. On a commercial level, he has also made his mark. It was Henry, let no-one forget, who turned the working man on to smelling lovely. One year, Fabergé made an advert called 'Henry Cooper's Christmas Party'. I was asked if I would like to take part, and when I said yes they asked me to be at Twickenham Studios at nine o'clock in the morning.

When I got there, at the beginning of a very warm June day, I found myself in a sea of familiar faces – Charlie Drake, Bobby Charlton, Bob Monkhouse, Kenny Everett and many more, plus pop stars, musicians… and Henry himself, who was flown in specially from Portugal on the Fabergé private jet.

Well, it was extraordinary. They filmed the whole thing like it was a gigantic Christmas party. I went into make-up at nine-thirty, and at ten o'clock I was on the floor. The set had been built to look like someone's home, complete with all the decorations – lights, paper chains and so on – and a big Christmas tree. A feller came up to me:

'What would you like to drink, Mr Tarbuck?'

'I'll have a cold lager,' I said, expecting them to produce a glass of lager-coloured fizzy water. But what he brought me *was* a lager. That day, all the drinks were real. And you could have as much as you wanted. More people arrived, and it was all 'Hello, boys. Have a glass of this. Champagne? Something stronger?'

At twelve-thirty, when we broke for lunch, everyone was as high as a kite and they hadn't got anywhere near my bit in the commercial. We went into the lunch room, feeling no pain, and there the wine flowed so freely it wasn't true. After lunch we went back into the studio and another hour or so floated by very pleasantly. At last it was time for my part, and I was sat on a couch with Charlie Drake. The Brut executive came up, followed by a camera and a sound man.

'Just talk about Brut for a minute, will you, boys?'

79

I turned to Charlie and said: 'We have a caddie at Wentworth who drinks Brut.'

'Oh,' said Charlie, 'and why is that, my darling?'

'He thinks he smells better when he farts.'

Charlie started to shake and squeal with laughter. I was laughing anyway – I hadn't stopped since about 10.15 and now it was the middle of the afternoon. Then up came Kenny Everett out of nowhere and smacked a cream cake over my nose.

'That's funny,' I said. 'I don't usually do impressions.'

They filmed the lot! And although they snipped out the caddie joke, the cream cake episode was used in the finished commercial. At about four o'clock they let us out, all well plastered. When I got home my wife took one look at me and said:

'Where have you been?'

I had nothing to hide. I gave it to her straight: 'Makin' a DV kershal,' I said.

'Oh, no you haven't!' she said.

The longest penalty

Another way to stay out of trouble – in theory – was to play in show-business football matches. If there was one thing you could say about the Showbiz XI, they were *competitive*. Talent was another matter. It was a bit like school in that way – you had people who could play and you had those who had no idea how to kick a football. Completely uncoordinated. Kenny Lynch, for instance, couldn't deliver a two-foot pass and get it straight. Tommy Steele thought he could play, and was great at the non-contact game; but once he was tackled, he was out of it. Then you had the really good pros who guested for us – people like Danny Blanchflower and Tommy Docherty who were, or had been, world-class international footballers.

There was a common bond between every member of the Showbiz XI – they all thought they were winners. Maybe it was the dressing up that did it for some, or the great venues we sometimes played, like Anfield or Ninian Park, Cardiff. There was the razzmatazz, too, and the wanting to look good, especially if the luscious Miss Diana Dors had just kicked off and might still be watching…

One game that brought out all the fever and hot-headedness of show-business football was a match between the Showbiz XI and the TV All Stars. It was a hard-fought game with feelings always threatening to erupt, and several harsh personal remarks were heard; to bring in the word

81

'vendetta' might be going a bit far, but the play was certainly spirited. With five minutes to go the score was 1–1, then the Showbiz XI were awarded a penalty.

Sean Connery came up to take it. A forceful figure, Sean was definitely the man for the job. Like many Scots, he knew his way round the football field – and he could also play. Sean placed the ball slowly and deliberately.

He was stepping backwards to measure his run-up, when suddenly there was a blur of movement. It was Dave King, one of the worst players ever to wear our colours; a completely hopeless footballer. A great bluffer, mind; he would come into the dressing room with three pairs of boots and ask if you thought he should wear the long studs, the short studs or the rubbers. Unfortunately, he couldn't kick a ball. Now he flew past Sean at the penalty spot, hacked at the ball and sliced it so wide of the mark that if the corner flag had been his target it might have been a good shot; as it was, I think he won a throw-in for the opposition.

There was uproar. Sean had Dave by the throat. 'What d'yer think yer doin'?' he snarled, with real feeling.

83

Dave had some trouble freeing himself, but when at last he could speak he looked up at Sean and in a voice of total seriousness said: 'You were taking too long.'

Nine members of the Showbiz XI fell about.

Last in the bath

The biggest charity football match I have ever played in was at Ninian Park, Cardiff, in aid of the Aberfan Disaster Fund which was started after the tip collapsed in the mining village of Aberfan and many, many children were buried in the schoolhouse. Bobby Moore, then captain of England, led our side and both teams were a good mixture of professional players past and present with a few show-business personalities like me. In the stadium there was a very moving atmosphere. A huge crowd sang the great Welsh songs, and in the middle of all those Welsh faces I remember spotting the Clark Brothers, Jimmy and Stevie, holding their trilbies over their hearts, singing away. I thought to myself: 'That's pretty good, especially from a couple of black American tap-dancers!'

The match itself was very entertaining for the crowd, with lots of goals and lots of incidents, and the show business element did their best to inject a bit of extra fun. About five minutes remained in the second half when the referee blew for a free-kick. The crowd, thinking it was all over, swarmed off the terraces and ran onto the pitch.

The referee decided he was going to have his own way, so he got the crowd off the field and eventually play restarted. A couple of minutes later, the ref was running alongside me. He said: 'I should get over towards the touchline, Jimmy, so you can get off quick and into the tunnel when I blow for time.'

So I got myself in that direction, and as soon as the final whistle went, I was off like a rabbit down the players' tunnel. As I scuttled in there, the crowd came roaring onto the pitch like the Russians at Stalingrad. I ducked out of trouble and got myself into the dressing room. I was the first in there. Great! Boots off, relax on the bench for a bit, then strip off and step into a big plunge bath. The others came in and did the same, and soon we were all immersed and having a wonderful soak while we chatted about the match and how well we had all played. We'd been in the bath for ten minutes or so when someone noticed that Tommy Steele wasn't with us.

'Hey,' went up the cry, 'where's Steeley?'

Nobody knew at the time, but he'd been mobbed by the crowd in the corner of the pitch. Just before the final whistle, the ball was passed up the wing; Tommy went after it, the referee blew for time, the crowd poured onto the field and Tommy was done for.

In the dressing room he still hadn't turned up. We got out of the bath, and were dry and changed, ready to go out to the coach, when in he came. Bedraggled wasn't in it; the cockney sparrow was in a terrible mess, the shirt ripped off him.

'Ere,' he said, looking at us. 'Where were you?'

'Where were we?' we all said. 'In the bath! And now we're going!'

'Get off,' he said. 'I 'aven't 'ad me bath.'

We all roared at him. 'No. And you're not going to,' we said, 'we've got to be at the station in a couple of minutes.'

Tommy was very disgruntled. 'It might seem funny to you lot,' he said, as we dragged him out to the coach. 'It's all right for you. Look what's happened to me.' He was still moaning pathetically when the train got to London.

XIII-a-side

As a tribute to my great knowledge of the game and well-known air of authority, they made me captain for one of the matches. I picked the team, and on the day thirteen arrived to play.

'Right,' I said, and drew up the team sheet. 'This is the first team and the two substitutes will come on later.'

'No we won't,' they said.

'What do you mean?' I said.

'We're here,' they said, so we play.'

There was a slight air of tension in the dressing room.

'That's nice,' I said. 'I thought I was the captain.'

'Suit yourself,' they said. 'Either we all play, or we don't go on.'

They were all against me. It was a palace revolution. I had to go along to the other team's dressing-room.

'Look,' I said to their captain. 'Have you got two more fellers who'd like to play, 'cos I've got thirteen and they all want to come on at the start.'

They found a couple more men. Someone told the referee, and a few minutes later twenty-six players took the field. In the crowd no-one seemed either to notice or care, and I later wondered how many players you could get on the pitch before someone complained. Forty? Sixty?

86

Railway pontoon

Many games of cards were played on these journeys. We were having a game of pontoon on the train one evening, when a couple walked past our compartment. I saw the lady pause, then she went on, came back, stopped and tapped on the window. Someone opened the door.

'Excuse me,' she said. 'We're Americans. I was just walking by and happened to look in.' She leaned towards a familiar blond figure. 'Are you Tommy Steele?'

Tommy nodded. 'Yes. I am.'

'Well, I saw you in *Half a Sixpence* on Broadway, and I very much enjoyed the show and your performance.'

So Steeley put his famous glow on, and showed her the teeth. (He's still doing it to this day. A lot of people think Shergar's back in show business – and I don't blame them. You see Steeley with those teeth and you don't know whether to shake hands with him or give him a lump of sugar.)

'Thank you,' grinned Steeley. 'That's very kind of you.'

The American lady peered round at the rest of us, sat there with the cards in our hands. 'Is this an English card game?' she asked.

'Yes,' we said.

'What's it called?' she wanted to know.

I said: 'It's called Bollocks Pontoon.'

'I beg your pardon.'

'Yes,' I said. 'Bollocks Pontoon. The way it works is, the players all try to get a hand which adds up to twenty-one. Isn't that right, lads?' The others were latching on. 'So, let's say I have a hand here. Add up the figures, and if it's twenty-one...'

'Bollocks!' roared the others.

'Well,' said the American lady, 'isn't that interesting.' Now she drew her husband in from the corridor. 'Look, Arthur, this is Tommy Steel whose wonderful show *Half a Sixpence* we saw on Broadway. He and his friends are playing a most unique card game called Bollocks Pontoon.'

We chatted for a couple of minutes longer and I learnt they were staying with an English family. Later I thought with delight of this nice lady saying to her English hosts:

'I met Tommy Steele on the train. He and his friends were playing a fascinating card game called Bollocks Pontoon...'

I wondered how that would have gone down in some Surrey drawing room!

Conversation at the Palace

Outings with the Showbiz XI were great fun days. The football matches we played were in a way the precursors of the charity golf matches that everyone now takes part in. The golf has even become international. Recently, a Great Britain and Ireland Show-business team played our American counterparts for the Duke of Edinburgh Trophy. I was made captain and picked a strong team of Celebs who could play. The others were James Hunt, Jerry Stevens, Kenny Lynch, Bruce Forsyth, Dickie Henderson, Eric Sykes, Sean Connery and Kenny Dalglish.

Before we all met up together, I said to them individually: 'I'll be doing the pairings soon, but before I do – are we playing this for fun, or do you want to win it?'

All except one man said: 'Let's win it.' So that was the attitude. We'd win the match – and have the laughs afterwards in the bar. I put the pairings together, and on the first morning we lost only one match – mine! Kenny Dalglish and I went down 2 and 1 to Charlie Pasarell and Richard Gere.

However, without going into further details, I don't at all mind telling you that we won the match. It was good to be able to fly the flag a little, and before it began, we went to Buckingham Palace to meet the Duke of Edinburgh. I introduced my team to him in turn, like they do on the pitch at Wembley before the Cup Final.

The Duke said to me: 'So you're captaining this lot?'

'Yes,' I said. 'Have you any tips on how to do it? You've captained teams before.'

'Well,' said the Duke, 'I've captained polo teams and cricket teams, but never a golf team.'

Eric Sykes chimed in: 'I've never been fond of polo.'

The Duke turned to him: 'Why is that, Mr Sykes?'

'That feller in the red hat,' said Eric. 'He never gets sent off.'

'Good heavens!' said the Duke. 'That's the referee!'

The Duke gamely persevered with the uphill task of talking to Eric: 'You were at the Palace six weeks ago, Mr Sykes.'

Eric thought about that for a bit. 'Yeees. Yes I was,' he said eventually.

The Duke added: 'You came for conservation.'

Eric stared at him. 'Oh no,' he said. 'I came for conversation.'

The Duke gave up and walked away. I followed, giggling. With a team like mine, how could we lose?

THE KENNY LYNCH STORY

Kenny and I played in a testimonial match at Liverpool for Gerry Byrne. Forty-odd thousand had turned out, and my team went on at half-time. When I ran on the pitch, the Kop shouted and clapped: 'Tarbuck for England – da-da de da-da – Tarbuck for England – da-da de da-da.'

When they saw Kenny Lynch they shouted: 'Eusebio! Eusebio!'

BABES IN THE WOOD

Pantomime has ancient roots, ancient jokes, and customs all its own. Since the Middle Ages, audiences have been hissing at villains and monsters, and their well-trained responses can be wonderfully sharp. So, at the Oxford Apollo in 1985, Cilla Black left a gap in her defences when, as Dick Whittington, she appealed to the audience:

'Boys and girls, how am I going to kill this terrible villain?'

A kid shouted out: 'Sing to him.'

Roars of laughter all round. And that is what is so great about this kind of live entertainment – no-one knows for sure what is going to happen next. The English pantomime is unique. My own experience as a performer began in Liverpool in 1964 as second top to Frankie Vaughan; then I did seasons at Coventry, the Palladium, Wimbledon and Birmingham, and made two pantomimes for television.

Life in the brief couple of weeks allowed for rehearsals is frantic, as each assorted bunch of performers gets to know each other and the script, while the producer, director and stage people combine to knock everything into shape, to make a little magic for the kids who are the main audience. Heading the cast is the star, who is probably a comedian or singer. Then there is the Dame, a specialist part which some like to make their own, spending six weeks to three months each year strutting about in voluminous drawers and a frilly bonnet, swatting giant rats with a rolling pin. My wife wants me to do a season as a pantomime Dame. She says it will give her a good laugh; I am not saying anything.

There may be other specialists in the cast – a horse built for two that has been doing the rounds for fifteen years; there was Richard Goolden who played Mole in *Toad of Toad Hall* until he was over eighty; there may be someone from a TV serial like *Coronation Street,* or a disc jockey, out to make his career 'blossom', as he might put it. Many surprises lie in wait for them all.

Pantomime has its special traditions, not least the one that requires the leading man to be a lady. A famous tale is told about a Coventry production of *Babes in Sherwood Forest.* The wife of the actor playing the Sheriff of Nottingham was living in London. One day she thought she would travel up to Coventry and surprise her husband. Surprise him she did. She found him in bed with Robin Hood!

The magic nuts

In the winter of 1964-65, Arthur Askey was my Mum. I sold the cow for threepence, and Arthur launched into one of his wonderful ditties:

'What, no milk?
Dear, dear, dear, dear.
This is getting quite a habit,
I shall have to milk the rabbit,
Dear, dear, dear, dear.'

Babes in the Wood

94

'Big-hearted' Arthur was a joy to work with, and both he and I loved a giggle. The show was a great success, ran for a long long time and was extended. For us, a long run was a mixed blessing, and we were all agreed that it was important to make our own bit of fun. If we had played the whole thing straight, word for word, day in day out, it would have driven us potty. I made it my aim to get some unscripted giggles out of Arthur. In the bar of the Palladium they had a collection of old theatrical bills, going back forty or fifty years to the heyday of music hall. I used to look at these bills – we had some others in our office – and picked out some likely names from long ago.

Arthur would be on stage with his sidekick, played by a lovely little man called Billy Tasker, when I came on.

'Good morning, Jack,' said Arthur.

'Oh, hello,' said I. 'Flack and Lamarr are looking for you.'

Flack and Lamarr were an old dancing act. Arthur and Billy, being two well-seasoned pros, latched on immediately, and started laughing. Another

95

day, mention of 'The Great MacGonachie' was enough to start them off. Or I might say:

'Scotch Kelly was down at the corner shop.'

Exit Arthur and Billy, twitching with private laughter. They could never understand where I got the names from, and I never told them.

One day Arthur said to me: 'I fancy an ice cream.'

We went round to the Italian ice-cream parlour where Arthur was a well-known customer.

'Ah, Signor Askey,' said the proprietor, picking up his scoop and a cornet with three compartments. 'An' whatta would you like today? I gotta vanilla, chocolata, caffè…'

'Yes,' said Arthur, 'I'll have that.'

So he put a scoop of coffee ice cream in the cornet. 'Strawberry,' he went on, 'raspberry…'

'Yes,' said Arthur, 'I'll have that.'

The proprietor put a scoop of raspberry ice cream in the cornet. 'Crushed nuts? ' he went on.

'No,' said Arthur, 'just a little rheumatism, as a matter of fact.'

Appearing nearby, at the Queen's Theatre in *A Servant of Two Masters,* was Tommy Steele, a confirmed practical joker. I was very green in those days; I knew nothing. At Simpson's in the Strand, Tommy asked me what I thought of the consommé.

'The what?' I asked.

Tommy indicated a bowl beside my place.

'Oh,' I said, and took a few spoonfuls. 'Bit cold, isn't it?'

Steeley was delighted. 'You berk!' he said. 'You've been drinking the finger bowl.'

One evening I went late-night shopping in the West End, and missed the half-hour call which goes out to make sure everybody is in the theatre thirty minutes before the curtain goes up. When I got back I found my understudy dressed in my clothes, all set to take my place. There was a very awkward silence.

'Oh,' I said at last, 'And what's this?'

'Oh,' they said. 'We had a call. Someone phoned in to say you had been run over in Regent Street and were taken to hospital with two broken legs.'

Tommy had set the whole thing up by telling me, hours earlier, that there was late-night shopping in Regent Street, and that Jaegers were selling cashmere sweaters for a tenner. Off I went, all innocent, for a browse round the shops. I stayed longer than I should have, but I wasn't worried because, although the half-hour call was at seven o'clock, I wasn't on until about eight, well into the show. At least, I wasn't worried until I heard I had two broken legs and concussion, and was laid up in a hospital bed! Thank you, Mr Steele.

Another little ad-lib, also from the Palladium pantomime. We had a full house for a matinee; a lot of matrons were in. I was on-stage, and the Princess came up to me.

'Oh, Jack' she said.

'Hello, Princess,' I said, and offered her a tin, which she had never seen before. 'I've brought you this tin of nuts,' I explained. 'I won them for you at the fairground.'

'Oh, Jack,' she said, 'how kind of you.'

'You're welcome, Princess,' I said. 'Would you like a nut?'

Game girl that she was – not that she had much choice – she opened the tin, there was a loud 'Whoooh', and out shot a rubber snake.

Well, I won't repeat exactly what she came out with, but it certainly wasn't in the script! '——————— hell!' may give you some idea. It had me crying with laughter, and so did the reaction of the audience. 'What was that?' I could see them saying to each other. 'What did she say?' 'No, she couldn't have. She couldn't have said that. Did she *really* say that?' It was wonderful. Drove the management wild.

Buttons in Italy
I was Buttons in *Cinderella,* working with the lovely Beryl Reid, one of my great favourites. Freddie Carpenter was the producer – a dear friend and the best pantomime producer of them all. After rehearsals one morning in Golders Green, Beryl said to me:

'Would you like a little lunch, Jimmy?'

'Yes,' I said. 'I would.'

So Buttons and this Ugly Sister went to an Italian restaurant round the corner.

'Have you had Valpolicella?' asked Beryl.

'No,' I said. I was still very young; I don't think I knew if you ate it or drank it or what –Valpolicella was still in finger-bowl country as far as I was concerned.

'I think you'll like it, dear,' said Beryl, as the first bottle of strong Italian red wine was brought to the table.

Well, to say that we imbibed would be a gross understatement. We started at a quarter to one, and were due back in the theatre at two o'clock. At ten to three, we stepped out into the daylight and wandered up to the theatre. I was very full indeed. We went in, and made our way down the aisle. From the stage, Freddie Carpenter glared down at us.

'Miss Reid!' he said, 'this is disgraceful.'

'Never mind that, darling,' said Beryl. 'Wait till you see Buttons. He's pissed!'

100

And I was. I was sent home for the rest of the day.*

*Shades of the Wilfred Lawson story in the 'Legless' chapter? Yes, and it happens more than once in a generation!

Flash Bang ... nothing

Frankie Vaughan and I were brothers in *Puss in Boots,* my first pantomime;
we were in Liverpool. The villain, our enemy, was a straight actor not
renowned – or so I thought – for his quickness. All his lines were delivered in
verse, and at one point in the performance he had me tied to a stake over a
trapdoor. According to the script, he spoke four lines, there would be a bang
and lots of smoke from the flashpaper which was worked electrically, and I
would disappear through the trapdoor. That fated night, the villain went into
his rhyme as usual:

> 'I have got a tale to tell.
> Puss will soon be down the well.
> And as for our young Sonny Jim,
> You have seen the last of him!'
> The villain pointed dramatically.

'Tssst!' – and I should have been on my
way. Unfortunately, the flashpaper
did not fire, because the
electrician who worked the
flashbox was not there. The
trapdoor half-opened, and
I slid down it and stuck,
with my head and
chest sticking up
through the floor.

I looked at the villain, and started laughing. He looked personally offended, and started the routine again.

'…And as for our young Sonny Jim,
You have seen the last of him!'

He pointed. 'Tssst!' Again the flashpaper did not work. The villain turned to me and quietly said: 'Egg on face', meaning that he was beginning to feel a right berk in front of the audience, who were now starting to enjoy our plight – as any self-respecting Liverpool audience would. So now he turned to face them and uttered these marvellous lines:

'Goodness gracious, what a caper,
Someone's pissed on the magic paper!'

He stamped off to huge applause. It was one of the greatest get-outs I have ever seen. True pantomime.

STARS AND SUPERSTARS

A great deal of rubbish is talked about stardom, whether in sport or show business. We live in an age of hype, and the newspapers and TV people have joined forces with the publicity agents to devalue the system. Nowadays any knock-kneed left back who plays for a team with its own pitch and a corrugated iron 'grandstand' will find the local paper calling him a star. He may like it, but where does that leave Kenny Dalglish?

In show business, the word 'star' is planted on people far too early – including me. I wasn't a star; I was a cheeky personality – the Sixties version of today's celebrity. Personalities, or celebrities, are not in the same league as stars – and sometimes don't want to be. Not everyone relishes the limelight. Some entertainers who could have gone on to become big stars have preferred to hang back and retain their privacy, not taking on more than they feel comfortable with. Stars are not like that: they have a hunger to be where the bright lights are, and to have a wonderful fuss made of them.

Stars qualify as stars in two separate ways. Firstly, they are

instantly recognizable. If you see Shirley Bassey in the street, or Ronnie Corbett, you don't have to think, you *know* who they are. The other qualification is through staying power. Stars must earn their stardom. If you look at the stars of British show business, they are people who have been at the top for twenty years or more. This is not meant to be a definitive list, but if you add to the names of Bassey and Corbett those of Max Bygraves, Bruce Forsyth, Des O'Connor, Cilla Black, Frankie Vaughan, you will see what I mean – people who have been in the public eye for a very long period, and who *enjoy* it.

For my own part, I can say firmly that the plusses of being well-known in show business far outweigh the minuses. Fame has opened a great many doors for me that otherwise would not have been open. And so it has for others. And allowed them to make the odd extravagant gesture. Bruce, for instance, has had a phone put in his car. Believe me, it looks stupid

with the kiosk sticking out the top!

Of course, being a star means you can get fans and total strangers chasing you at night. Cilla was coming home from a television recording. It was late, and as she drew up at a set of traffic lights a feller tooted at her: 'Beeb-beeb' and called out: 'Cilla!'

Cilla's husband Bobby was driving and she said to him: 'Drive on, Bobby. I can't stop now for autographs.'

They drove on until they were stopped at another set of traffic lights. The feller drew up alongside: 'Beeb-beeb. Cilla!'

'Drive on, Bobby,' said Cilla, looking straight ahead and taking no notice of the feller.

This happened about five times; on each occasion the feller tooted and called out, but Cilla refused to acknowledge him.

'Drive on, Bobby,' she said. 'I'm not saying hello to this feller.

Hasn't he gorrer home to go to?'

The more Cilla ignored the feller, the more frantic he seemed to get. He shouted at her, beeped his horn in longer and longer bursts, flashed his headlights – no good, she wouldn't take any notice.

At long last Cilla and Bobby got away from the feller and drove home. When she got out of the car, she noticed something that explained a lot. Her full-length fur coat was hanging out the door and they'd dragged it all the way home from the TV studio!

The Jewish Mercedes

Stars usually have star cars, which they acquire on the way up the ladder. Rolls Royces are a popular choice, and very nice too, though maybe a little ordinary nowadays. There was a time, not so long ago, when star cars stood out more, and some were stars in their own right.

In the late Fifties a Jewish screenwriter called Marty Rackin lived in California. He bought a Mercedes, a fine-looking car, but was surprised by the resentment it drew from his Jewish friends.

'How can you buy a German car?' they asked him.

'I like it,' he would answer. 'It's a fine car.'

'It's a *German* car,' they said, with hurt in their voices.

Marty didn't want to sell the car, but he didn't like being responsible for the upset it was causing his friends. He decided to change the emblem on the front of the bonnet. He had the Mercedes device taken out and replaced with a chrome Star of David.

Now when his friends and business associates rode in the car, they looked down the bonnet... and couldn't believe their eyes.

'What's this?'

'That's the emblem,' Marty would say. 'This car was made in Israel.'

'How is that possible? A German car made in Israel?'

'Yes,' said Marty, who had rehearsed his story. 'After the war it was part of the reparations imposed on the Germans that they should open a special factory in Israel and Mercedes cars would be built there under licence. This is one of them. The Star of David is what sets them apart from other Mercedes.'

The word spread, and soon Marty was renowned as the man with the Jewish Mercedes. But now, instead of reproaching him, people were more likely to say: 'Hey! Where can I get one of these cars with the Star of David?'

Starbuck and COMIC

Pat Henry was a great American comic, now sadly passed on. His nickname for me was 'Starbuck', for which I take no credit. He was appearing with Frank Sinatra at the London Palladium, and after the show Pat and I were going out for a meal.

Outside the theatre he saw a car with an unusual numberplate: COM IC.

'Jesus Christ!' said Pat. 'Look at that.'

'Sure,' I said. 'Get in.'

'You sonofabitch!' he yelled. 'It's yours.'

Some weeks later I was over in Palm Springs. A Mercedes drew up outside the hotel; in it was Pat, and the numberplate said COMIC.

'You sonofabitch!' I said to him. 'What's that?'

He looked, for him, quite bashful. 'Yeah,' he said, flapping a hand as if to dismiss it. 'Well, I thought it was like a good idea..'

He had wasted no time at all. Luckily for him, in the States they can put on more or less whatever number they want – unlike here, where it can cost an arm and a leg just to have your own initials, let alone COM IC.

Frank who?

So much for star cars. Now it is time to look at some superstars. Earlier in this chapter I said that stars have two things in common, and one is that they are instantly recognizable. Superstars share this quality – it almost goes without saying – but they have something more, a kind of magic aura which surrounds them. It is extraordinary, and unmistakeable when you come into contact with it.

Superstars are not usually to be found walking the streets, especially not in the United States where most of them live. But they are available to be seen, if you know where to look. I wasn't looking at the time. I just walked into the Tamarisk Country Club and there was Frank Sinatra sitting with Andy Williams – two in one look!

With them was Pat Henry. 'Starbuck', he called. 'Come over'. I went over.

'Starbuck', said Pat. 'I told these two bums that you're doing a tour and you might need a singer on the bill with you.'

I bottled out – one of the few times in my life when I could think of no quick exit. 'Thank you very much, Pat,' I spluttered and waited for someone to change the subject.

'Whassa matter with you?' Pat demanded. 'You gone chicken?'

'That's all right,' I muttered. 'I think we have a singer already booked.' To myself I thought: 'Jeez, why does he do this to people?' Andy and Frank, meanwhile, just looked at one another and smiled. Superstars.

My first meeting with Frank Sinatra came about through George Raft, that great star of a thousand gangster movies. George was over in London running a club while I was compering *Sunday Night at the London Palladium,* and I had him on the show a couple of time. Various rumours were going round about his underworld connections and I cannot comment on them; I only know that he was a great guy to be with. He was also something of a hero with my old man, because of the movies. One night I took my Dad into George's club. I told George I was coming in and he said: 'What's his name?' I said: 'Fred.'

We went into the club and George Raft came over. 'Freddy,' he called to my old man. 'How are you?'

The old man was a picture of surprise and delight. 'Oh, hello, George!' We sat down and the people at the club treated us like royalty. A great night.

I was over in the States for a TV show, *Jackie Gleason's Birthday Spectacular,* and staying in Miami at the Fontainebleau Hotel (pronounced 'Font'n Blue'). A guy came up to me:

'Jimmy Tarbuck?'

'Yes.'

'The man wants to see you.'

I said: 'What man?'

He said: 'Frank.'

I said: 'Frank who?'

He said: 'Sinatra.'

Well, I was up out of my chair, changed and ready in two minutes flat. I went downstairs and was shown into a room – and there he was.

Sinatra said: 'Hi, Jimmy. I believe you looked after George in England. Well done.'

He was a big Raft fan, too. I sat with him and we had a terrific evening. Later we went on Ben Novak's boat. He owns the Fontainebleau Hotel and his boat is called *Fontainebleau 2.* It's a beautiful boat, wonderfully furnished, slightly smaller than the *QE2* but not so you'd notice. Ben Novak showed me several of its finer points:

'Ya know Heals, in London?' he asked me. 'We got da drapes from Heals. Da table's from Harrods. So's da lamp.'

I expressed admiration. We sat down on a bench seat; me next to Sinatra. I was like Bostic with him that day; wherever he went, I went. A waiter came up:

'What would you like to drink, Mr Sinatra?'

Sinatra said: 'I'll take a Jack Daniels on the rocks.'

'And you, Sir?' asked the waiter, turning to me.

I said: 'I'll take a Jack Daniels on the rocks.'

Why I said that I don't know; I guess it must have been the Bostic Factor at work. I had no idea what I was ordering. I was still very much in my show-business youth, and a Jack Daniels could have been Tizer, dandelion and burdock... you name it, I would have said: 'Great stuff, this Jack Daniels.'

Sinatra looked at me: 'Uh-huh,' he said. 'A Jack Daniels man.'

I said: 'Oh yes.'

'I didn't think you could get it in England.'

'It's a little difficult,' I said, as if I had exclusive knowledge.

Along came the waiter with the glasses. Frank and I took our Jack Daniels.

'Here's looking at you,' said Frank.

'Psschoo!' I said, after taking a too-quick gulp of raw Bourbon and spattering some of it round the deck.

'Oh, sorry Frank,' I gasped. 'A little chesty today.'

It might have been the bullshitter's come-uppance, but Sinatra was charming and allowed me to regain my composure and, you might say, carry on posing, because that day I was gloriously full of myself, inebriated by the mere idea of Here-I-am-having-a-Jack-Daniels-with-Frank. A wonderful day.

Even the great stars take a night off occasionally. Tony Bennett, of *San Francisco* fame, was throwing a party at his home. The doorbell rang and young Master Bennett went to answer it. There stood the jazz trumpeter, Dizzy Gillespie.

'Hi,' he said. 'I'm Dizzy.'

Young Bennett looked concerned. 'Come in and sit down. I'll get you a glass of water.'

Tony Bennett swears this is true!

111

Ah! Grimsby…

One man whose voice I have enjoyed imitating on more than one occasion is the great Welsh singer Tom Jones – who recently left his body to medical science, except for one part which is going to the Hall of Fame!
Many years ago we had a memorable night together in the Midlands. I was in a pantomime in Coventry and he was in a show in Birmingham.

After the panto, he sent his car over for me and I went to Birmingham to watch him. He finished his show and we had a few drinks

together. The night went on, turned into tomorrow, and at about six in the morning we drove back towards Coventry.

There was snow on the ground and we passed a group of fellers waiting for a bus to take them to work. We pulled in at the bus stop and lowered the dark-tinted windows of Jonesy's car, a big black Rolls. I called out:

'Where the bloody hell have you lot been till this time of the morning?'

It got a great response. Snowballs everywhere, thudding into the car. We made our escape and got back to the hotel in Coventry. At this point our schedules proved to be very different from each other. We were both knackered, but whereas Jonesy could sleep all day – I called him Count Dracula and he seemed to like it – I had to get up and do a matinee.

'Ave a good show,' laughed Jonesy, 'I'm gonna have a good sleep now'. And he shut the door of his room.

'Rotten bastard,' I thought, and rang Reception. 'Mr Jones 'ere,' I said in my best Valleys accent. 'Will you send me up a nice grilled trout.'

The trout was cooked and taken up to Jonesy's room while he slept on. For about five hours he and trout rested in the same room, but while Jonesy was growing steadily fresher as the minutes passed, the trout was doing the opposite. In the centrally heated stillness, the smell given off by the fading trout went from a mild fishiness to a foul and dreadful stench, penetrating the curtains, the carpet, the bedclothes . . . and finally pushing up into the nostrils of Mr Jones with sufficient force to wake him.

'Bloody 'ell! What's this?' he shouted, and rushed from the room.

Now, of course, Tom Jones is a superstar on both sides of the Atlantic – even more so over there, which is rare for a British performer. I was over in Las Vegas while Tom was appearing there, and very much wanted to see Elvis Presley who also had a show. But the queues were unbelievable. They ran all the way back to Los Angeles. There was no way of getting in by queueing for a ticket. I would also add, since this is a book about show business, that the Presley show was the greatest example of how to sell a performer that I have ever seen. Outside the hotel it didn't give his name. All the publicity said was: 'HE'S HERE'. As you walked in the hotel, there were banners everywhere – even in the gambling saloons; there were giant teddy bears with his song ('Just wanna be your . . .') emblazoned on them, and every member of staff wore a straw hat with Elvis's name on. This was all Tom Parker's doing: a wonderful piece of hype and salesmanship, the immediate result of which was that I couldn't get in.

I went on one of the house phones, and in an American voice said: 'Hi. What's the name of the Maître d' in the main room?'

'Mr Carlo,' came the answer.

'Thank you,' I said, then put the phone down and picked it up again.

'Ello,' I said, 'Tom Jones 'ere. Can you get me Carlo in the main room?'

On he comes. 'Tarmmmmy! How are ya?'

'Ello,' I said. 'And 'ow are you, Carlo?'

'Well, Tarmy, it's really nice to talk to ya...'

'Look, will you do me a favour? I've got a mate and his wife. Jimmy Tarbuck, 'e's called. Can you find 'im a table?'

'Send him to the front, Tommy. He'll have the best seat in the room. And tell him not to worry about any expenses. That will be our pleasure, Tommy. We will see he gets champagne.'

'That's very nice of you, Carlo,' I said.

'Leave it to me, Tommy,' boomed Carlo.

I walked round to the front with my wife, Pauline, who was shaking her head in disbelief. I went up to someone in the foyer.

'Is Mr Carlo...' I began.

'Mr Tarbuck? From England?'

'Yes.'

'Go right through, please.'

We strolled in, turning our backs on the huge queue. We were shown to the best seats. Champagne arrived. It was truly wonderful.

In the presence

The next night, with Tom, we were taken to Elvis's dressing room. To say I felt in awe is an understatement. There I was, about to meet this guy whose records I had bought since I was a kid. The next minute, out he came. This was before he put the weight on, and he looked great. The King. Not the best-dressed man I have ever seen: he wore a white suit with four black pockets and a black velvet collar. But undoubtedly the King of Rock & Roll.

'Hi,' he said. 'I'm Elvis Presley.'

I introduced myself and my wife. We spoke for a while, and Elvis was great company. The next night, I saw him again. He came into

114

AYUNTAMIENTO DE TIAS
LANZAROTE

Con motivo de las cercanas fiestas Navide-
ñas, esta Alcaldía se dirige a todos los veci-
nos y visitantes de nuestro Municipio, con
sus mejores deseos de paz prosperidad.
Para dar realce al marcado carácter festivo
de las celebraciones. alegres y populares se
ha preparado para el próximo 31 de Diciem-
bre. en la Avenida de las Playas y en la zona
de la Playa Blanca, una exhibición de fuegos
artificiales para congratularnos de la llegada
del año nuevo, a las 24,00 horas.

¡FELICIDADES!
EL ALCALDE

Zu dem Kommenden Weihnachts fest und
Neujahr wünscht das Bürgermeisteramt
von Tias, allen Bewohnern und Gasten frohe
Weihnachten und ein glückliches Neues Jahr.

Um das Neue Jahr zu begrüssen, findet am
31 Dezember um 24⁰⁰ Uhr and der Strand
strasse und an der Zone von Playa Blanca ein
grosses Feuerwerk statt.
Wobei Sie alle herzlichst eingeladen sind.

DER BÜRGERMEISTER

To the Christmas and New Years day the
Mayorship of Tias wish all the people and
Guests Merry Christmas a happy New Year.
So, Tuesday 31 of December at 24⁰⁰, we
make for all our people and Guests at the
beach street and Zone of Playa Blanca a big
fireworks and every body is invite.

THE ALCALDE

Tom Jones's room, and I told a few gags and he laughed. He was so good to be with, I can't believe all this crap that's been written about him since he died. It's become the in-thing to destroy people who have become myths as soon as they're out of the way and can't answer.

At the end of the evening, Elvis stood up in the middle of a very crowded dressing room and said goodnight to all the ladies. 'Goodnight, ma'am, Goodnight, ma'am.' He went round every lady in the room. He didn't have to. He could have gone to the door and called 'Goodnight, folks', like anyone else. No-one would have minded. He chose to do it in the old Southern style. The ladies' knees may have turned to jelly, or they may not, but they will always remember the time Elvis said goodnight to them personally. I thought: 'You'll do me. Superstar.'

THE KENNY LYNCH STORY

Kenny drew an unfortunate rebuff, what I call a double-blank, with Mick Jagger.

We had been to see The Rolling Stones at Wembley Stadium. It was a massive concert, with over seventy thousand people there. The Stones put on a great show, and afterwards we all went to Tramps. I knew Bill Wyman well, also Ronnie Woods, but I didn't know Mick Jagger. When he came in, he was very hoarse from the show. I said to him:

'Great. That was great tonight.'

'Oh,' whispered Mick. 'Thank you, man. Yeah.' And smiled.

Kenny was next to me. He got a blank from Mick, who just gave him a quick nod – no sign of recognition – and turned away.

Another night, Kenny and I were in Tramps when Mick Jagger came in with some other fellers and sat at the next table. One of them called across to Kenny:

'Hi, Kenny. How are you?'

Kenny talked to him for a bit and introduced me. Then the feller turned to Mick and said: 'That's Kenny Lynch over there.'

Mick went: 'Oh, yeah,' with no enthusiasm at all. So that was another knockback. Not a big one, but enough to put Kenny out. He had had a few drinks, so he leaned towards the feller he knew and said:

'You just tell Rubber Lips that me and my mate here are earning... bundles!'

I roared. It tickled me so much that ever since I have called him Bundles Lynch.

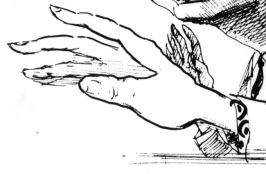

THE LAST LAUGH

In this book I have taken a small tour round the byways of show business, and most of what we have seen is true. But what has show business meant to me? First of all, it has meant having a wonderful time meeting so many great people in an industry which, as I said earlier, almost seems to defy analysis.

If I can ever describe the mysterious appeal of my profession, it is probably summed up by a meeting I had one day at Bertram Mills Circus. I was invited behind the scenes and there I found a feller mucking out the elephants. I stood there with a handkerchief over my nose in the humid atmosphere as he shovelled and swept his way through the latest deposits. When he paused to rest on his broom for a moment and mop the sweat from his face, I asked him how much he earned for his work.

'Fourteen pounds fifty,' he replied.

'What!' I said, 'I'll pay you twice that to come and work in my house as a handyman.'

'Oh,' he said. 'I couldn't, guvnor. No, I couldn't give up show business.'